HARDIE AND BAIRD
& OTHER PLAYS

By the same author

An old pub near the Angel, and other stories
Three Glasgow Writers (with Tom Leonard & Alex. Hamilton)
Short Tales from the Nightshift
Not not while the giro, and other stories
The Busconductor Hines
Lean Tales (with Agnes Owens & Alasdair Gray)
A Chancer
Greyhound for Breakfast
A Disaffection

HARDIE AND BAIRD
& OTHER PLAYS

JAMES KELMAN

Secker & Warburg LONDON

This collection first published in Great Britain 1991
by Martin Secker & Warburg Limited
Michelin House
81 Fulham Road
London SW3 6RB

A CIP catalogue record for this book
is available from the British Library
ISBN 0 436 23289 8 (hb)
ISBN 0 436 23287 1 (pb)

Printed and bound in Great Britain
by Clays Ltd., St Ives plc

for all the Roughcast team

Contents

Foreword

In this country arguments against public funding for the arts are usually irrational and decisions to cut or withdraw subsidy are always political, greed being the ultimate motivation. This is illustrated by the folk in current power, locally and nationally, who pretend to various philosophic absurdities, while doling out massive sums of public money to private enterprise. Mutual self-interest amongst an exclusive few is once more the mainspring of government, and the term 'teamwork' carries its own moral force. The idea of the arts operating on both public and private subsidy suggests a heady mixture of high principles coupled with sound business sense. It can further imply that left to their own devices those already engaged in the field are not quite up to the more mundane practicalities. They might hold lofty ideas to do with morality, aesthetics, the human condition, and so on and so forth, but when it comes to making a thing 'work' they need help from more down-to-earth sort of chaps. Art is all very well but out there in the real world it is a fight for survival.

The battle has been on for a while, people struggling for private funding, trying to tempt open the sponsor's purse; some winning, some losing. The evaluative criteria employed by those in control of this purse are not known to myself. Predicting motivation is more straightforward. But it seems safe to suggest that the art most likely to 'win the money' will conform to certain precepts deriving from these criteria and will be decorative rather than challenging. Anything too radical or experimental or in some sense 'geared to a minority audience' begins with a handicap, as does the work of an unknown artist, sculptor, painter, playwright or whatever.

Like any successful product, a work of art should be acceptable to as wide-ranging a market as possible, 'market' here referring to media-response as much as potential audience. If a subsidised theatre company or gallery is doing its job properly, that is, in line with current philosophy, then 'sponsor-appeal' exercises an influence on its commissioning of plays, events or exhibitions. A theatre company no longer approaches a group of small sponsors for various bits and pieces connected with the production itself: nowadays an initial cash injection is crucial. The *predicted* criteria of potential private funding bodies thus come to form part of the theatre company or gallery's *own* criteria for judging the worth (rather than merit) of new work. Its value is therefore determined by its potential 'sale' to the private sector. A 'difficult' play is no longer a challenging piece of original drama, it is one deemed worthwhile by the company's management but thought unlikely to find major funding from private sources.

Perhaps with a lot of hard book-balancing work and various cost-cutting exercises a company on public subsidy can succeed in producing one play without major sponsorship per season, but perhaps not. The Traverse Theatre in Edinburgh is one of the ever-dwindling band of companies still trying to cope. But what is happening in the arts is happening everywhere else public funding is essential, especially in those areas where whatever benefit or profit there is remains in the hands of the public. In our society profit is supposed to be private, only the costs are public.

When a theatre company wants to produce a so-called 'difficult' play but cannot entice a private funding body to subsidise the enterprise it is left with one or two alternatives. Offering a 'workshop' production is one of them. This immediately breaks through the public subsidy 'barrier'. Any publicly funded arts body must abide by certain agreements, one of which guarantees the artist a minimum fee for her or his work. On a 'workshop' production the playwright has the freedom to choose either a token fee or else no fee at all. It further solves the 'union problem': the company need not pay its members to the minimum Equity rate. In fact, they need pay no wages at all, only expenses. A 'workshop' production does not offer the ultimate exercise in cost-cutting, which is voluntary liquidation, but it does mean great savings all the same: no rehearsals, no set, no sound, no lighting. The actors have the freedom to choose to wear their own clothes or no clothes at all, and stand about on the stage with manuscripts in hand and do a sort of performance reading.

Obviously there are drawbacks: nobody has the remotest sense of being involved in an actual play; and for the audience (who frequently have to pay at the door for the privilege) the experience is not quite as good as being present in a recording studio when a radio dramatisation is taking place. 'Workshop' is a way of paying lip-service to original work and new writing. Few companies like doing it. One which maintains full production interest in a 'difficult' play might feel entitled to wonder if an element of 'script-liberation' could broaden its sponsor-appeal, i.e. can the manuscript be adjusted slightly to make it that bit less off-putting to the folk holding the purse. So as well as controlling initial decisions on the production of new work the private sector quickly comes to exert influence on 'script-development'.

What it comes down to is imposition, the imposition of external value on criteria that should be the province of art and aesthetics. This is true to the point of banality for those writers, directors, actors and others engaged in dramatic art forms within film and television; and a short answer for the depressing state of affairs in either medium, where to describe current output as second-rate is generally taken as a compliment. The folk with the money take control.

One obvious, though seldom acknowledged, correlate of the shift from public into private sector arts subsidy is the increase in suppression and censorship. It is hard to imagine a dramatisation of the offshore oil workers' fight for improved safety conditions being sponsored by any of the major oil companies; as hard as it is to imagine US corporate funding for a realistic portrayal of its entrepreneurial activity in Central America or the Middle East, or anywhere else for that matter. And oppression leads to repression; the situation where writers and artists stop creating their own work. They no longer see what they do as an end in itself, they adopt the criteria of the 'market-place'; they begin producing what they think the customer wants. At this stage the customer is no longer even the audience, nor is it the commissioning agent of the actual theatre company; the customer has become the potential sponsor, the person holding the purse strings on behalf of private business interests. What the artist is now producing has ceased to be art; it has become something else, perhaps a form of decoration, or worse.

People engaged in the arts continually make decisions on whether or not to continue working at what they do, even where it becomes possible to survive economically at it; one reason being that the vast bulk of the work on offer is geared to the needs of private sector money. Such work is not only meaningless but often in direct conflict with the artist's own motivation. Some hold out by entering extended periods of 'rest'; others try for a compromise; they do the hack stuff and trust the money earned 'buys time' for more meaningful work in the future. For those who persevere on their own account the mediation between themselves and economic survival is eroded.

Of the three plays in this collection **Hardie and Baird: The Last Days** was produced by the Traverse Theatre in Edinburgh, a part-subsidised company still in existence, battling to stage 'unsponsorable' work. There aren't many left. The other two were produced by a company operating on what is described as a 'profit-share basis'. Thus when Roughcast Theatre produced **The Busker** and **In the Night**, in lieu of payment, actors and backstage members of the company worked as a co-operative, sharing the profits on a points system at the end of each run. This is possible when a company receives no public subsidy and is therefore entitled to the freedom to choose to work for nothing or not to work at all. For the benefit of government agencies funded to observe the arts at a microeconomic level, individual actors at the top of the points system received some £80 for seven or eight weeks' work, *including* expenses, i.e. a return on their outlay for travel etc.

As playwright and thus prime mover of both 'profit-share' enterprises I did feel slightly guilty on occasion but only slightly. And nor do I take the view that the right to exploit must exist in any free society and that those who are exploited are so by their own free will. It is simply the case that folk involved in the performing arts, in company with most other people, would rather engage in meaningful work for nothing than not work at all.

Many of those within the higher income bracket in Britain express concern at the hardship endured by artists. They assume the group is part of their own and therefore empathise with them; 'That could be me', they think. Others from the same income bracket are not depressed, they take the more aggressively romantic line and accept the necessity of suffering for art's sake. They do not for one minute think 'that could be them' but believe in the freedom to starve. Members of either faction assume artists receive their just reward at some indefinable point in the future, in the form of cash or glory, perhaps posthumously. If some artists never succeed in 'winning a reward' from society at all then they couldn't have been worth rewarding in the first place; perhaps the work they produced wasn't very good; perhaps it was 'wrong' – maybe it just wasn't Art at all – for within these circles of conventional left as well as right wing thought the myth that art with a capital 'a' is both product and property of society's upper orders is taken for granted. A line emanates from the same mentality which is often assumed to derive from a 'class position'. Members of this group accept the foregoing myth wholeheartedly and denounce Art as elitist, and all of those engaged in its creation self-indulgent time-wasters.

I am not opposed to art 'dirtying its fingers in the market-place'; nor am I in favour of it. The question is irrelevant. What is at issue is value, whether or not we allow art (or culture) to be judged by the yardstick of private profit-making bodies.

There are those who maintain that an Age of Liberalism existed in this country from the mid 1960s until a time in the mid 1970s. This may or may not be true; it is probably true for those who assume that the British Broadcasting Corporation was once an instrument for freedom. But art and subversion are close allies anyway so the notion that creative endeavour has a right to public – let alone private – subsidy is something of a contradiction. It is much more consistent that people engaged in the field as an end in itself should be attacked in one way or another, for this is a time of punishment, out there in the real world.

James Kelman
(Glasgow, 1990)

THE BUSKER

The Busker was written for actor/musician Alan Tall whom I have known and been friends with for a number of years (we recently discovered we went to the same secondary school in Hyndland, Glasgow). The play derives from a short story of mine but took off somewhere else altogether once I had him in mind for the role – I knew that I could rely on his grasp of wherever I was at in the music, which is quite particular to a certain aspect of the 'sixties. **The Busker** was first produced by Roughcast Theatre at the Assembly Rooms during the Edinburgh Festival Fringe of 1985; cast as follows:

Busker	Alan Tall
Ponce	John Cobb
Lady	Katy Duke

Directed by Ian Brown
Musical arrangement by Alan Tall
Design by Minty Donald
Stage managed by Alison Goring
Administered by Peter Kravitz
Photographs by John Gilmour
Drawing of cast by Alasdair Gray

NB 'For **The Busker** I played a 1972 Guild D35 acoustic guitar with D'Addano medium gauge phosphor bronze strings (J17 set, 056–013, currently £5.65). The action was high and I fingerpicked hard, using brass bridge pins for sustain, though I don't know if they made much difference. I used normal tuning a semitone down from concert pitch, using a brass Shubb capo to compensate. I also used DADGAD tuning (semitone down) and for "If Not For You" DGDGBE (semitone down) which I flatpicked hard and sang loud. My picks were Hero nylon flatpicks and a clear plastic thumbpick.

'I smoked 3 Castles tobacco from an old plastic Old Holborn tobacco pouch with Rizla green papers and Swan Vestas for matches. From the audience my doctor friend, Helga Rhein, diagnosed bronchitis early in the first tour but I can't recall which antibiotic she prescribed.

'I've been listening to Doc Watson, Bob Dylan, Del Shannon, John Lee Hooker, J. B. Lenoir, Bert Jansch, John Renbourn, Ralph Towner and Egberto Gismonti on and off for years now. I haven't busked since Paris 1968.'

Alan Tall
(Glasgow, 1990)

Cast

Busker   Man in his mid thirties
Ponce   Smaller man: a couple of years older
Lady   In her early thirties

Notes on direction:

This play is written for actors at home with the Glasgow accent; but they should not feel constrained by the words on the page, nor by the directions on movement. The actor in the part of **Busker** must be competent on the guitar.

Scene   A Birmingham pavement
Time   Around noon on a dry winter's morning
Music   As directed
Props   Acoustic guitar. A pebble. A piece of silver paper. A tobacco tin and pouch etc.
Lighting   As directed

Act One

Sound: Tape begins prior to lights: it is a piece for guitar, preferably played by **Busker** *himself – country/folk/R & B. Then it finishes and tape switches into* **Busker** *playing 'Candy Man': continue for no more than a minute or so.*

Lights: Not too brightly.

Busker *is in his position up/centrestage, probably tuning his guitar. The empty tobacco tin lies to his front. When ready he picks up on 'Candy Man' from the tape, and gradually fade out tape, leaving* **Busker** *on his own.*

Ponce *eventually appears sidestage during this song. He lifts something from the ground and examines it, sticks it away into his side jacket pocket – probably a smooth pebble, nothing of monetary value. He is preoccupied by what he is doing, unaware of* **Busker**'s *presence though he does hear him play. He listens for a moment. Then notices something glitter on the ground, he steps towards it, nonchalantly slow in his approach, glances sideways and casually picks it up.*

Ponce (*immediately*) Fucking silver paper! (*Screws it up.*) Dirty bastard! (*Shake of the head as he flicks it to the ground, attempts to dropkick it but misses, shakes his head again.*)

Lights: More brightly.

Ponce *continues strolling round downstage, pausing to listen. He smiles, enjoying the performance, nodding his head and otherwise displaying his appreciation. His awareness of the audience is his awareness of other pedestrians. Eventually* **Busker** *stops playing and* **Ponce** *seems to be watching closely as though to see whether or not the 'pedestrians' drop in coins. No one does of course.*

Busker *brings his tobacco pouch out from his jerkin pocket, unzipping it he begins rolling a smoke.*

Ponce (*walks towards him, but not too directly, taking his hands out his trouser pockets and blowing into them: he gives a twitch of the head by way of a greeting*) Aye, bad time of the year for this game eh! The weather man, fucking murder!

Busker *doesn't acknowledge his presence, still rolling the smoke.*

Ponce Aye, carols, it's carols you should be giving them! (*Glances around at audience.*) This time of year man that's what they're looking for: carols!

Busker (*sniffs*) Yeh jock.

Ponce (*cheery surprise*) What was that!

Busker Carols . . . yeh. Could be right jock, you could be right.

Ponce The accent man! Jesus christ! What a relief! A London voice on a Birmingham pavement heh! Where you from?

Busker London's right.

Ponce No kidding! Well well well. Well well well right enough! London eh! Whereabouts?

Busker *frowns for a moment, sticks roll-up in between his lips.*

Ponce In London I mean, whereabouts? Whereabouts in London?

Busker Oh. (*Nods.*)

Ponce No Old Holborn eh!

Busker *puzzled glance at* **Ponce** *who indicates the cigarette.*

Ponce Naw it's the tobacco, the tobacco; it's the tobacco I'm talking about man it was a joke, know what I mean . . . ! (*Points at the cigarette and takes an imaginary one from his own mouth, does an imaginary exhale of smoke.*) The Old Holborn and aw that!

Busker *nods casually, takes the pouch back out from his pocket and tosses it to* **Ponce** *who catches it quite easily.*

Ponce Aw thanks, thanks, thanks a lot man I mean I wasnt eh you know, eh . . .

Ponce *shrugs.* **Busker** *nods.* **Ponce** *takes a paper from the Rizla packet inside and starts rolling.* **Busker** *has got his matchbox out, strikes the match, gazing vacantly about, disinterested in everything.* **Ponce** *still rolling, not wholly successfully. But when finished it is sufficiently well rolled to smoke. He speaks before finishing.*

Ponce Long you been here?

Busker *shrugs.*

Ponce A while?

Busker Nah, not really jock . . . (*Peers at the cigarette* **Ponce** *is now licking and preparing to smoke, smiles.*) Alright?

Ponce What . . . ? Yeh, aye . . . My fingers just, a wee bit numb. The cold. (*Holds the cigarette with a flourish. And* **Busker** *throws him the box of matches without comment. Again* **Ponce** *catches it easily.*) Ta. (*Strikes match and lights cigarette. Throwing back the matches he* *enters a real coughing fit.*) Oh jesus christ almighty, jesus christ almighty, oh jesus . . . (*Ends in a short bout of sneezing, during which he sticks the fag away in his pocket, unnoticed by* **Busker**, *and the majority of the audience.*)

Busker Alright mate?

Ponce (*brings out a big hankie*) Just give the nose a wipe . . . (*And proceeds to do so.*)

Busker *watches him for a moment, then begins footering/tuning the guitar, his interest in* **Ponce** *waning.*

Ponce Aye, christ. (*Another wipe of the nose, returns hankie into his pocket.*) It's that first drag of the day man always the same so it is. (*Glances at* **Busker**.) Nectar but. Nectar! (*Smiles, glances at tobacco tin, steps a pace towards it.*) So how you doing? You earning? (*Reaches his leg out to give the tin a gentle kick: then moves to look straight into it.*) Forty fucking pence!

Busker (*shrugs*) Yeh jock, bleeding hopeless.

Ponce Aye you're no kidding! Christ, what's up?

Busker (*a bit taken aback*) What's that?

Ponce (*gestures at tin*) Naw, I'm just meaning cause you've only made that much. Forty pee! I mean christ . . . !

Busker *shrugs, smiles briefly. Pause.*

Ponce Forty fucking pence but I mean that's murder man, murder, fucking terrible.

Busker Yeh. (*Still footering with guitar, now turns slightly away from* **Ponce** *and begins the next song, a slow blues.*)

Ponce *smiling. He becomes aware of audience, gazes at them as though trying to gauge their interest in the music. Eventually he strolls slowly to the side. Then he notices a 'pedestrian' appear and his gaze follows the 'pedestrian' across the stage, passing* **Busker**, *and he watches the tobacco tin.*

Busker *is not aware of anything* **Ponce** *does here; he is engrossed in the performance.*

Ponce (*gazes after another 'pedestrian', loses interest. Then another 'pedestrian', whom he watches pass the tobacco tin and he frowns and shakes his head, mutters*) Miserable bastard . . . ! (*Then he calls:*) Gone ya miserable bastard ye! (*Renewed interest as another 'pedestrian' appears, and this one also seems to ignore the tobacco tin.* **Ponce** *shakes his head and cups his hand to his mouth to call:*) No appreciation! (*Glances at* **Busker** *who doesnt notice. Then he watches another 'pedestrian', and mutters:*) Fuck sake. Miserable bastards! Miserable tight bastards! (*Frowns and gets onto his feet, squares shoulders and rearranges his shirt collar, buttons up his jacket, and walks towards* **Busker**, *and swiftly bends to lift up the tobacco tin.*)

Busker *amazed look at what is happening, a very very slight break in his playing.*

Ponce (*hand cupped to mouth, a loud whisper*) I'm just going to do the business. Know what I mean? (*Indicates 'pedestrians', rattling tin a little.*) I'm just going to do your collecting!

Busker *just looks at him, continues looking as he plays on.*

Ponce (*turning to audience, glancing into tin, pokes a finger in to check contents. Then his attention drawn to the next 'pedestrian' coming from sidestage and sets off to meet him, begins rattling tin, and speaks without humour*) Couple of bob for the singer john, eh, couple of bob for the singer? (*Walking backwards.*)

Busker *frowns.*

Ponce (*now grins at a 'pedestrian', rattles money in tin*) Right you are, ta, thanks, thanks a lot. (*Dodges forward to rattle tin under the next 'pedestrian's nose'.*) The singer missis, couple of bob for the singer . . . (*Grinning.*) Thanks, thanks a lot. (*Gazes after her a moment then winks at* **Busker**, *gazing again as though at the woman's legs, resumes on the next 'pedestrian'.*)

Busker *shakes head, eyes close, but still continues playing: opens his eyes and directs song at audience, ignoring* **Ponce**'s *actions.*

Ponce (*walking backwards again, rattling tin, then dodges slightly and turns to call*) Gone ya miserable bastard ye! (*And to* **Busker**, *jerking his thumb after the 'pedestrian':*) The cunt's probably a millionaire as well! (*Grins and returns to the fray. The next along are two female 'pedestrians' and he walks backwards, glancing from one to the other, rattling tin.*) Ah come on dear eh? Couple of bob for the singer. Eh? Come on! Come on! Eh? (*Points at* **Busker**.) Heh – this is a poor forgotten son of song you're talking about, he used to make records! Naw, no kidding ye! (*Rattles tin and laughs briefly.*) Well done, ta, thanks a lot! (*Follows another 'pedestrian'.*) Couple of bob for the singer john couple of bob for the singer! (*Slightly more aggressive now.*) Ah come on for christ sake, eh!

Busker *now watching him again, he stops singing and continues on the guitar alone.* **Ponce** *rattles tin as if he has just received something*

from someone: turns to the next 'pedestrian'. Meanwhile **Busker**
brings the tune to a natural conclusion, and stops playing.

Ponce (*is unaware and rattles tin again*) Eh missis? Eh . . . (*Walks
backwards a moment, then notices* **Busker** *has stopped.*)

Busker *strikes match to light the old roll-up he was smoking earlier
but doesn't get it burning properly, and he chips it away in a vaguely
irritated fashion. He brings out his pouch, is soon rolling another
smoke quickly, all the time watched by* **Ponce.**

Ponce Aye, you've been doing that a while!

Busker *glances at him and sniffs, breaks match in two, drops it onto
the ground.* **Ponce** *still holds the tobacco tin in his right hand, raises
his cupped left hand to his mouth and he blows into it, heating
himself: he turns slightly to gaze into the audience, watches
'pedestrians' pass by. He then looks at* **Busker** *as though wondering
what is to happen now, but without making it too obvious.*

Busker *ignores him. He leans his elbows on the guitar, relaxing,
enjoying the smoke.*

Ponce (*gives a twitch of the head, and generally*) Aye! Fucking cold
yin this morning! (*Raises cupped left hand again, his right hand also
moves and the money rattles inside the tin, and he looks at it and
sniffs, glances at* **Busker**.)

Busker (*returns the glance, continues to gaze at him for a moment*)
Can you sing jock?

Ponce What . . . ?

Busker Can you sing?

Ponce Can I sing?

Busker *just nods, inhales and exhales.*

Ponce Eh . . .

Busker No?

Ponce Eh naw, naw . . . (*Sniffs.*) It's no that man eh . . . no really, I'm
no into that eh country and western stuff, no really, I'm no really
into it.

Busker Blues jock, blues. (*Quick glance sideways as though to make
sure nobody is listening.*) I dont sing that country crap. (*Clears throat
as if to spit, but doesnt. He glances at* **Ponce**.)

Ponce (*eventually*) Aye. (*Nods. Sudden smile.*) I've been trying to
sing that 'Swiss Maid' for years! (*Still smiling, but taking for granted*

Busker *knows what he's talking about.*) Del Shannon man you heard of him?

Busker (*vaguely*) Yeh.

Ponce Maybe a bit before your time right enough.

Busker *shrugs.*

Ponce It's these fucking yodels beat me. I just canni get them. (*Shakes head, smiles briefly, then speaks/sings.*)

> One time, a long time ago
> On a mountain in Switzerland yodel odel oh
> There lived, a fair young maiden
> Lovely but lonely yodel oh oh
> One day, her papa said, you'll go
> Down from the hills in the valley

(*Stops.*) Ah! Fuck it! (*Dismissive wave of the hand. Looks at the tobacco tin, then walks a pace to lay it on the ground like it was before.*)

Busker *now walks downstage and peers out over the heads of the audience, to see a clock on a high building.*

Ponce (*squints after him*) Time is it?

Busker Getting on jock, getting on . . . (*Pause. He glances at* **Ponce** *while returning to his stance.*)

Ponce I can sing that 'Kelly'.

Busker *nods, drags on his fag.* **Ponce** *awaits a reply. Then he blows into his cupped hands, rotates his shoulders, gazes at passing 'pedestrians'.*

Ponce Aye, I'd give it a go, I'd give it a go.

Busker *lodges cigarette in the corner of his mouth, rubs hands together briskly, then begins strumming quietly.*

Ponce I mean if you played the tune man . . . (*Watches* **Busker** *strum a moment or two.*) I'd give it a bash.

Busker (*sudden frown, glances at him*) What's that jock? (*Stops playing.*)

Ponce 'Kelly'. I'm saying I'd give it a buzz man, I'd give it a go, if you played the tune I mean . . . (*Shrugs.*) It's up to you – if you wanted . . . it's up to you. (*Sniffs.*)

Busker (*resumes strumming, then calls*) You know any Dylan jock?

Ponce Dylan?

Busker Yeh.

Ponce Course.

Busker *nods.*

Ponce Aye . . . Bob Dylan, aye. (*Shrugs.*) Only problem I find with him man is the words and that I mean I dont mean they're bad and that man I just eh what I'm talking about, trying to remember them man, that's what I mean, the way sometimes you dont remember them man, the words – you ever find that? I mean you think you know the fucking things and then you start to sing it, and do ye! Do ye fuck! (*Snorts.*)

Busker *nods, but isnt interested, checking guitar keys now.* **Ponce** *still awaits response from him.* **Busker** *now picks out a tune and becomes engrossed in it.* **Ponce** *watches intently, genuinely interested. He glances at audience surreptitiously, then looks at the tobacco tin. He then addresses* **Busker**:)

Ponce I'll give it a go but! Something by Bob Dylan. Okay? I'll give it a go!

Busker *looks at him, still playing.*

Ponce (*raises his voice a little*) I'm saying I'll give it a go man – something by Bob Dylan, okay – what will you play the tune or what?

Busker (*pauses in play, adjusting his attention*) What was that jock?

Ponce What're you ready? (*Sniffs, gives a twitch of the head.*)

After a moment **Busker** *shrugs.*

Ponce I'll sing that yin eh . . . (*Frowns.*) Christ! (*Grins and snorts.*) Canni even mind its fucking name now!

Busker *waiting for it.* **Ponce**'s *face screwed up.*

Ponce Eh . . .

Busker Just you sing it. (*Pause.*) Just you sing it.

Ponce (*frowns*). Bare you mean?

Busker *nods.*

Ponce *also nods.*

Busker (*pause*) And I'll follow in mate, alright? Once you've started off. You just start off. Alright?

Ponce Eh aye, okay, okay. (*Unbuttons his jacket, adjusts his shirt collar and prepares himself, then turns and shouts, but as though trying to be quiet at the same time.*) 'Tambourine Man' it is!

Busker Right jock.

Ponce (*clears his throat. Concentrates, adjusting his breathing, begins an internal count to five, then begins singing, gazing over the heads of the audience*)

> Hey Mister Tambourine Man play a song for me
> I'm not sleepy, and there aint no place I'm going to
> Hey Mister Tambourine Man play a song for me
> (*. . . And so on*)

This song should not be sung as any sort of parody. **Ponce** *is doing his best, and* **Busker** *is not at all ironic, nor is he disassociating himself from it in any way whatsoever. But gradually it becomes wayward through* **Ponce**'*s failure with the words, he becomes repetitive, then hums to fill in the bits he doesnt know, and then he gets self-conscious, becoming more aware of the 'pedestrians'.* **Busker** *is meanwhile doing his best given the circumstances.*

Ponce *eventually tails off into silence. He gazes around, controlling his self-consciousness. He makes a display of watching a female 'pedestrian' pass by, and to* **Busker** *in an aside*) Nice wee arse on that eh!

Busker *doesnt respond. He has continued playing alone, and glances at* **Ponce** *only when he has brought the tune to a conclusion.*

Ponce (*pause. He clears his throat and shrugs, gestures at the tobacco tin*) It was better with me just doing the collecting.

Busker *gives an ambiguous nod of the head, tunes guitar, or pretends to.*

Ponce Eh? We no just better sticking to that? (*Pause.*) Eh? What about it man, what do you think? We no better sticking to that? You do the singing and the rest of it and I'll hold the box? Eh? I mean at least we were getting a fucking turn that way! Eh?

Busker *is non-committal.*

Ponce Eh? What d'you think?

Busker *begins picking out a tune.*

Ponce (*now outshouts the instrument*) No fancy it?

Busker What's that jock?

Ponce I'm saying if you just do the singing man while I'm doing the collecting, know what I mean, we were doing alright . . . (*Nods.*) We were doing alright . . . (*Indicates the tobacco tin.*)

Busker Nah! (*Continues picking the tune.*)

Ponce (*shrugs*) You could even just do that man, the instrumental; you dont need to bother singing.

Busker Songs they like jock!

Ponce Yeh . . . (*Grins.*) This time of year man that's exactly what I was saying – fucking 'Jingle Bells'!

Busker *smiles and does some sort of flourish with the 'Jingle Bells' tune.*

Ponce Brilliant! (*Laughs.*) That's brilliant! No kidding ye man I mean all ye need to do is the instrumental. I'll get the dough off them. No danger. (*Grins and makes the move to lift the tobacco tin.*)

Busker (*sudden command*) No!

Ponce (*halts immediately. After a moment he speaks ironically*) Very sorry . . .

Busker (*sniffs, peers at him*) Much I got there jock?

Ponce (*nudges tobacco tin with his toe, checking the contents without actually going so far as touching the money*). Two quid I think nearly, about.

Busker Yeah?

Ponce (*nods*) About two quid.

Busker (*appreciative*) Mmm.

Ponce Aye.

Busker Not bad, not bad.

Ponce That wee lassie, her with the yellow coat, she dropped in fifty pee! (*Grins.*) I think she must've fancied me! Rare pair of legs she had on her as well did you see them?

Busker *doesnt respond, attending to the guitar keys again. Pause.*

Ponce Heh! Fancy a couple of rolls or something? Eh? Ye hungry?

Busker *shakes head.*

Ponce Pork pie or something?

Busker Just had me breakfast jock!

Ponce (*echoing*) Breakfast!

Busker Yeh.

Ponce Breakfast . . . Hh!

And now **Busker** *picks out another blues, in an engrossed manner, as though not especially busking. He continues for a time, with* **Ponce** *just watching, uncertain whether or not* **Busker** *is playing for 'real' – then eventually* **Ponce** *decides he isnt and calls*:)

Ponce I'll tell you something man, I've no eaten for days – days. I'm talking about days, and I'm no kidding ye!

Busker *ignores him, continues playing.* **Ponce** *laughs wryly.*

Ponce Bar a tin of fucking sardines. That's the whack man, that's it, a tin of sardines. No kidding ye man that's the fucking truth, that's all I've had. Terrible! (*Moves restlessly when* **Busker** *doesnt respond.*) Naw I mean that's how when you talk about breakfast . . . (*And now he shows irritation.*) Tell you something for nothing man you and your fucking breakfast man I mean christ! Breakfast! (*Shakes head.*) I mean you dont know, you just fucking dont know. Understand what I'm talking about? (*Turns abruptly, he is facing the tobacco tin. He goes and lifts it.*)

And immediately **Busker** *stops and stares.* **Ponce** *replaces it at once, and addresses* **Busker** *angrily*:

Ponce What's wrong with you christ I was just going to do a bit of collecting, eh, I was going to do the business, that's all – what's wrong with ye! something wrong with ye!

Busker *shakes his head and resumes playing.*

Ponce (*aggressively*) What's wrong with you at all eh? is there something wrong with you!

Busker *turns slightly away from him and* **Ponce** *glances sideways at passing 'pedestrians' and continues in a loud angry whisper*:

Ponce I'm asking if there's something wrong with you?

Busker Leave it out jock.

Ponce Leave what fucking out? (*When* **Busker** *ignores him he circles to face him directly.*) Leave what fucking out?

Busker *glances at him.*

Ponce Listen a fucking minute, if it wasni for me you'd still have forty fucking pence. Forty fucking pence. Cause that's all you had till I arrived, forty pence!

Busker *stares at him while bringing the music to a quiet close. And* **Ponce** *looks away, less aggressive now.*

Ponce Naw man, no kidding ye, if it wasnt for me you'd still just have forty fucking pence.

Busker (*sniffs and steps back to lean against the wall, taking out the tobacco pouch, speaking as he does so*) Yeh jock yeh. Yeh, I know all that, I know all that, if you hadnt've come along I'd still be out there a bleeding pauper, yeh, I know all that . . .

Ponce Yeh well aye, you'd still have forty pee man that's all I'm saying – they were giving you fuck all till I arrived and started doing the business, the collecting and aw that.

Busker (*making the cigarette as he speaks*) Doing the collecting, yeh, well that's the bleeding problem jock innit, too heavy.

Ponce How d'you mean?

Busker Too heavy. Ten more minutes of you and the Man'd be here, sticking me for extortion.

Ponce The Man?

Busker Yeh jock the Man. (*He licks the gummed edge, passes the finished roll-up to* **Ponce** *and makes another for himself.*) Too heavy . . . Aint the way. Just no good jock just no good. (*He continues now and finishes the second cigarette, brings out the matches, gives the first light to* **Ponce**, *lights his own.*) Yeh, extortion they call it.

Ponce You're talking about the Busies . . .

Busker That's it, yeh.

Ponce (*puffs briefly on the cigarette, frowns and walks a pace or two, glances sideways, turns to speak*) I mean it's no as if I was touching them man I mean christ almighty I mean I wasni fucking threatening them or nothing . . . (*Glances sideways again.*)

Busker Yeh . . . (*His attention now to the guitar, and* **Ponce** *shoves the cigarette into his jacket pocket.*)

Ponce (*glancing sideways, mutters*) These bastards are paranoiac . . . (*Hands into trouser pockets, watching a couple of 'pedestrians' pass, turns to* **Busker**, *looks at him for a moment.*) Aye I mean . . . (*Sniffs and gazes sideways, gazes after a 'pedestrian', glances at the tin, then* *at* **Busker**.) Heh eh look man, I think eh, I mean, I think I'm christ due something I mean eh. (*Twitches head in direction of tobacco tin.*)

Busker (*immediately*) Take a sov.

Ponce (*hands aloft in refusal gesture*) Naw naw I'm no due that . . . The fifty pee just, I'll take the fifty pee.

Busker Take the sov jock.

Ponce (*pause. Frowns*) You sure?

Busker nods. **Ponce** *waits a moment, then also nods.*

Ponce Aye well okay then but I'm starving man, really, no kidding ye. Fucking ages since I've ate anything . . . (*Lifts tin, counts contents by poking his finger about inside. He takes the amount in coins and displays the money to* **Busker** *who nods, returns tin to the ground.*) Listen eh I was going to say . . . you wanting anything yourself? A roll and sausage or something?

Busker Nah jock, if it's all the same.

Ponce You sure.

Busker Yeh.

Ponce I mean it's no bother, it's no a problem, if you wanted something . . . Heh what about a pint of milk then? Or tea! A carton of tea, what about a carton of tea man there's a cafe sells ye carry-outs just round the corner eh? A cup of hot tea man it'll heat you up and that for fuck sake ye must be freezing, your hands and all that, numb, must be about falling off for fuck sake . . . ! (*Gestures at guitar.*)

Busker (*genuine response*) Yeh jock, a drop of tea, that would be nice. Yeh.

Ponce Aye christ no bother . . . (*Pause. He glances at tobacco tin again, then at* **Busker**.) Cup of tea eh?

Busker Nice, yeh.

Ponce (*nods, sniffs; indicates money in his hand*) I'll get it out of this.

Busker nods, not looking at him. He starts to play and sing another blues. **Ponce** buttons his jacket up, adjusts his shirt collar.

Ponce I'll be back in a minute then!

Busker *gives a slight nod without interrupting the playing.* **Ponce** *pauses again, then makes to leave.* **Busker** *gazes after him, then his* *attention wholly on the music.* **Ponce** *nods, turns and dodges as though to avoid bumping into a 'pedestrian'.*

Ponce Sorry missis. (*Continues on and exits.*)

Busker *plays on, engrossed in it.*

Lights fade after a time and the music switches to a tape version of the same, and fade out on that, both lights and sound simultaneously if possible.

Act Two

Lights and music simultaneously. **Busker** *is playing a slowish song by Bob Dylan, in a slightly different position from previously.* **Ponce** *enters, hands in trouser pockets, casually strolling. He notices* **Busker**, *saunters on downstage and peers in the direction of the clock on the 'high building' opposite and over heads of audience.*

Busker *has spotted* **Ponce** *while continuing the song, but he too squints as though to see the time.* **Ponce** *turns slowly and calls:*

Ponce How ye doing? (*A greeting rather than inquiry.*) Alright!

Busker *ignores him completely.* **Ponce** *continues strolling, occasionally glancing at 'pedestrians', then casually glancing at the tobacco tin.* **Busker** *now bringing song to a close.* **Ponce** *smiles in a friendly manner.*

Ponce Aye, earlier on man, just after I left you, I bumped into this mate of mine's, hadnt seen him for a couple of weeks, wound up I had to go a message and that and while I was away there was this big pile up and that, crowds of folk . . . (*Tails off.*)

Busker *interrupts somewhere towards the end of the last sentence as though playing a concluding verse to the last song, but perhaps without singing.*

Ponce (*mutters*) Bastard!

Ponce *walks off a pace or two, hands still in trouser pockets. And* **Busker** *ends the piece with a low-key flourish.* **Ponce** *turns to him.* **Busker** *now alters his stance a little, facing away from* **Ponce** *more, towards opposite sidestage, where* **Lady** *has appeared unseen by anyone other than* **Busker**, *and he launches immediately into another song, this time a cheery uptempo one of Dylan's – 'New Morning'/'If not for you' as possibilities.*

Ponce *gets down on his hunkers (sits on his heels). He sees a crumpled piece of paper and lifts it, flings it away; rubs his hands, cups and blows into them, is attracted by a 'pedestrian' and follows her/him with his gaze. He now begins enjoying the music, keeps time by nodding, still rubbing his hands etc., sees a 'pedestrian' drop some coins into the tin, smiles.*

Lady *has been here for an indefinite period, but in walking a pace or two forwards she now appears in view. It is probable that* **Busker** *switched tempo because he had spotted her at the outset of the song* *but this should remain probability only.* **Lady** *is clearly enjoying the music, she carries a handbag and maybe it swings a bit to the rhythm.*

Ponce *is the last person in the world to spot her and he is amazed then delighted, and takes a step towards her.* **Lady** *either hasnt seen him or ignores him absolutely, and she begins quietly clapping to the music, but she* isnt *uninhibited.* **Busker** *is now engrossed in his playing again and takes no notice of either.*

Ponce (*moves another step closer to* **Lady**, *calls*) Yeh, he's good!

Lady (*without looking at* **Ponce**) He's bloody brilliant. (*Pause, and to* **Busker**:) On you go! (*Slight irony.*)

Busker's *attention drawn to her once more.*

Ponce (*delighted by her ordinary Glasgow accent, and he laughs briefly*) You're from Glasgow?

Lady *ignores him.*

Busker *now making plain his awareness of her, turning slowly while singing, as if playing for her alone, with humour, just enjoying her presence and her own enjoyment. Eventually* **Lady** *closes her eyes, rocking a little with the rhythm.*

Ponce (*glances from one to the other, begins a mild clapping to the beat, notices a 'pedestrian', continues the mild clapping: he is trying not to be excluded from the others' relationship – but not blatantly so. He calls to* **Lady**) Aye he's good him, he's definitely good: the McCoy!

Lady *still ignoring him, her eyes closed, is now occasionally joining in on the song, the line endings, so that she is heard to know it without knowing it too well.* **Busker** *continues to sing and play seriously. Eventually* **Ponce** *too attempts to join in, the word at the end of the line etc., although he had never heard the song in his life before this.*

Lady *lowers her handbag to the ground, clapping more freely. Immediately* **Ponce** *glances at the handbag, then at* **Busker**, *and at the audience/'pedestrians': there is an air of guilt about* **Ponce**, *as though he anticipates someone accusing him of contemplating the theft of the handbag.*

Busker *brings song to its conclusion, and he faces audience with another low-key flourish: he gives a brief laugh and shake of the head, turns away and brings out his pouch, prepares a smoke.*

Lady (*smiles*) That was great . . . (*To nobody in particular. A pause and she looks at* **Ponce**, *then looks at her handbag.*)

Ponce (*after a moment*) Aye, he is good him – makes you wonder how he's still playing at street corners!

Lady (*slow nod*) Ah well, some you win, some you lose.

Ponce Aye, true, true enough. (*Smiles – just glad she's spoken to him at all.*)

Meanwhile **Busker** *smokes in the background, quietly observing the dialogue, but not with much real interest.*

Lady (*almost to herself*) Some people dont bother.

Ponce Aye . . . (*Expecting further comment.*)

Lady (*studies him*) You got a fag?

Ponce Eh aye, yeh, yeh . . . (*Fumbles in side pocket.*) Somewhere . . . (*Straightens it out before handing it to her.*)

Lady A roll-up. (*Examines it.*) It's been lit . . . !

Ponce Eh aye . . . (*Sniffs.*)

Lady *shrugs, puts it in her mouth, holds palms upwards to him.* **Ponce** *stands, puzzled. Pause.*

Lady You no got a light?

Ponce Aw aye. Aye. Hey you got a match there man? (*To* **Busker**, *and he walks towards him.*)

Busker *casually tosses him the matchbox which he catches with less ease than before.* **Lady** *has walked a couple of steps behind* **Ponce** *and he turns to her, strikes a match, tosses the matchbox back to* **Busker**.

Lady (*to* **Busker**, *shrugging*) I'm smoking roll-ups now. (*Exhales a cloud of blue, not really inhaling much.*)

Busker *smiles non-committally.* **Lady** *indicates* **Ponce**.

Lady So's he right enough. (*Wry smile at* **Ponce**.) We all are . . . I liked that song you sang there.

Ponce Dylan.

Lady (*sideways*) Yeh. (*Glances back at* **Busker**.)

Busker Thanks. (*Glances sideways, now maybe disassociating himself.*)

Lady (*notices her cigarette isnt burning*) Bloody thing's gone out.

Ponce (*when* **Busker** *doesnt respond, calls firmly*) Heh man, you got a light there?

Busker *looks at him and sniffs, flings him the matchbox.* **Ponce** *drops it [or catches it with a little difficulty] and eventually gives her a light, tosses the box back to* **Busker**.

Lady (*exhales a cloud of smoke again. Smiles to* **Busker**) You should be on records! You know that? Well you should be, you should be on records. Top of the Pops . . . ! (*Ironically. She dances a couple of steps and laughs quietly.*)

Ponce *also laughs, delighted by her.* **Busker** *nods vaguely, and* **Lady** *frowns at him.*

Lady I'm serious but. I am. You're definitely good enough. (*To* **Ponce**:) Isnt he?

Ponce Aye christ. Course they're no wanting good singers on the telly. Same with records and that, they're no interested. Maybe if he was in a group or something.

Busker *smiles, but unnoticed by other two. Pause.*

Ponce (*to* **Lady**) Course you've got to get the right songs and that I mean, if you've no got the right songs . . . eh, I mean, you'd be as well chucking it. There's too many into it.

Lady (*vaguely*) Yeh, I suppose . . .

Ponce (*shrugs*) It's like everything else.

Lady Mmm. (*Pause. She glances at* **Busker** *and turns, noticing 'pedestrian' pass, then she laughs to herself, briefly, and twirls her hand aloft, and laughs to herself again: then turns abruptly to* **Ponce**, *frowns.*) What's that one again? (*Shuts her eyes a moment.*) That one eh . . .

Ponce What?

Lady That song. (*Opens her eyes.*) I'm trying to mind a song I used to like . . . (*Gazes at him.*)

Ponce Eh . . .

Lady Oh God it's eh . . . Tch.

Ponce It'll come to you. (*Pause.*) I mean is it a new one or what?

Lady (*ignores him. She sighs*) Tch! (*Twirls her hand aloft and calls:*) Mamma cara, Mamma cara! (*As in Mamma mia.*)

Ponce *puzzled.*

Lady (*sighs, still ignoring him. Now she glances at* **Busker**, *displays her roll-up*) Hey have you got a decent smoke there at all Charlie?

Busker (*waits before replying*) I'm rolling them love. (*Polite, but keep-your-distance.*)

Lady I did notice. You're no a Birminger, a Birminghammer eh?

Ponce He's from London. He's a Cockney. (*Smiles.*) And you're from up the road yourself eh?

Lady (*sighs*) More or less.

Ponce (*when no further comment comes*) So what you doing down this neck of the woods?

Lady (*looks at him*) What do you want to know for?

Ponce Pardon?

Lady I'm saying what d'you want to know for?

Ponce How do you mean?

Lady (*turns to* **Busker**) He's like the bloody polis isnt he!

Busker *grins.*

Ponce Me?

Lady Aye. You. (*Unsmiling.*)

Ponce *glances away, looks to* **Busker** *who doesnt respond.* **Lady** *closes her eyes, holds her hands palms upward and sings:*)

Lady I'll be with you, in apple blossom time . . . (*Opens her eyes.*) My mammy used to sing that. (*Stating a fact, no trace of maudlinity.*)

Busker *begins tuning the guitar.*

Ponce Your mammy?

Lady (*ignores him, then to* **Busker**) Hey you where's your case?

Busker What's that love?

Lady Your case. For your guitar. (*Looks about.*) You no supposed to have one? I thought yous usually kept them there so's the people could put in their money?

Busker Yeh.

Lady You no got one?

Busker No.

Lady You did have one but eh?

Busker Uh-hu.

Ponce Did somebody knock it?

Busker (*now looks straight at* **Ponce** *for probably the first occasion since the opening of this scene*) Yeh jock, as a matter of fact.

Lady Aw that's awful.

Ponce Was there money in it at the time like?

Busker No.

Ponce (*nods*) Was it out in the open or what?

Busker What's that?

Ponce Naw I mean your case and that man, for your guitar, when it got knocked, was it out in the open or what? Was it in the house?

Busker (*sighs and squats: sighs again*) How d'you mean jock?

Ponce Naw, I'm just wondering eh, if it was out in the open, daylight, I mean when you were actually working, if you were singing at the time.

Busker *gazes up at him.*

Lady (*turns on* **Ponce**) See you and your questions! I'm no kidding ye, you're worse than the bloody polis!

Ponce What! Me? Naw I'm no, wait a minute, what you talking about? Not at all, christ – what d'you mean?

Lady *draws him a look. She glances at her roll-up which went out a while back, she flings it away.* **Ponce** *stares after it, blows into his cupped hands, looks at her.* **Lady** *now opens her handbag and searches inside, but closes it without finding anything. Her attention attracted by 'pedestrians'. Turns to* **Busker***:)*

Lady You're missing all the folk.

Busker Yeh; well. (*Shrugs.*)

Lady (*smiles*) Come on; get up and start playing.

Busker Ah!

Lady (*indicates audience*) You've no time for sitting on your behind.

Ponce She's right but man: everybody going by you's going by you – understand what I'm talking about? All that money? (*Grins.*)

Busker *ignores him.* **Ponce** *studies him, wondering if* **Busker** *'isnt talking to him'.* **Lady** *loses interest, turns and walks side/downstage, stares off.*

Ponce (*to* **Busker**) Naw but no kidding ye man I mean the lady's right, you dont earn the wages by sitting on your arse . . .

Busker (*rises somewhere during the last line, glares*) Where's me tea jock?

Ponce Your tea . . . ?

Busker Yeh me fucking tea jock.

Lady *turns to observe.*

Ponce (*nods his head in direction of* **Lady**) No need to swear man – christ, I just forgot.

Busker (*mutters*) Yeh.

Ponce (*calls to* **Lady**) His tea! I was going to bring him a carton of tea, and I forgot.

Busker Yeh you forgot!

Ponce (*angrily*) Aye I forgot aye, big deal eh. Big bloody deal.

Busker Ahh! (*Shakes his head in disgust.*)

Ponce What will I go and get it the bloody now or what!

Busker (*studies him for a time*) I wish you'd just fucking piss off altogether mate. Yeh, I wish you'd just fucking piss off.

Lady (*sighs, murmurs*) Oh oh . . .

Ponce (*aggressive*) What d'you mean?

Busker You're a ponce mate, that's what I fucking mean! (*Turns away.*)

Ponce (*stares at him for a full five seconds*) Dont fucking call me a ponce.

Busker *ignores him.*

Ponce Heh you! (*Loudly.*) Dont you fucking call me a ponce. (*Wags finger at him.*) Hey you, I'm talking to you!

Lady (*moves a couple of steps towards him, finger to her lips, loud whisper*) Sssh . . . (*Indicates 'pedestrians'.*)

Ponce Ah well him! (*Dodging round her to confront* **Busker**.) Calling me a ponce like that and I'm fucking doing the business man that collecting I'm fucking there doing it man that collecting, the fucking tobacco tin, and he's turning round and calling me a ponce! A fucking ponce! Fucking calling me a ponce, know what I'm talking about, a fucking ponce! (*Genuine disbelief as well as rage.*)

Busker *puffs on his fag but it has gone out.* **Ponce** *stands stiffly, staring at him.* **Lady** *observes. Then* **Ponce** *moves as if to resume the verbal attack.*

Lady (*checks him with a movement*) Hey . . .

Ponce Ah well, well, it's no bloody fair, it's no bloody fair. (*Turns from her to stare out beyond audience, turns slightly to the side.*)

Busker *glances at his guitar keys, begins footering with them.*

Lady (*walks a pace to* **Busker** *quietly*) Hey you, surely you're a bit out of order? Eh? Surely . . . I mean he was doing your collecting.

Busker *frowns at her.*

Lady (*sighs and laughs quietly to herself, twirls hand in the air, dances a step*) Mamma cara! Mamma cara . . . (*Glances back at* **Busker**.) Come on you, Charlie, give us a song – come on.

Busker (*angry but keeping control*) Look love this is my work, alright, my work, my bleeding work I mean I'm trying to bleeding work here, you know? Work?

Lady (*faces him squarely*) Aw now listen pal dont start that kinda patter with me!

Busker *stares at her.*

Ponce (*turns and points, calling*) I mean he canni even fucking sing! That's the best of it. It wouldnt fucking matter if he could sing, but he canni, he canni! (*Walks towards them.*) Okay he's no a bad guitarist, fair enough, okay – but see they fucking songs he sings they're rotten. Aw jesus christ. Jesus christ! They're fucking rotten, they're rotten, no kidding ye, fucking rotten!

Busker (*angrily fumbling his tobacco pouch out his pocket, and fine if he should drop it in the process*) Yeh! Yeh! Well just fucking piss off then you cunt, just fucking piss off!

Ponce *just stares at him.* **Busker** *stares back, then resumes with the pouch and the preparation of a smoke; the process calms him down.* **Ponce** *now gazes at the pouch.* **Lady** *also watches the process.* **Ponce** *glances at her and* **Lady** *gives him a look, and he turns away.*

Lady (*sighs. She also turns, steps downstage in a self-absorbed manner, closes eyes, begins smiling to herself, then she calls to* **Busker**) Hey, can you play any reggae?

Busker What's that lady?

Lady Can you play any reggae? (*Pause. Does a couple of dance steps.*)

I love that reggae . . . (*Sighs. Laughs to herself, then starts to sing with her eyes closed*:)

> Red red wine . . .
> Stay close to me
> All I can be

(*And continues, swaying as she sings.*)

Ponce (*grinning*) On ye go hen! On ye go!

Lady's *sway/dancing becomes more sensual. She doesnt know all the words but she hums in tune, becoming quieter, more self-absorbed.* **Ponce** *is smiling, rapt.* **Busker** *is also rapt but gradually he becomes aware of the 'pedestrians' and tries to distract her. But* **Lady** *is unaware. Eventually he calls softly:*

Busker Hey love . . . better watch it eh . . . (*Nods in direction of audience.*)

Lady *now notices him and is a little self-conscious, but not unduly, and when* **Busker** *holds the rolled cigarette to her she walks forward to get it.*

Lady (*takes cigarette and looks at it.* **Busker** *has begun rolling another*) Aw no one of these again!

Busker *is taken aback.*

Lady (*grins*) I'm only joking. Honest, I'm only joking.

Ponce *is watching closely.* **Busker** *continues rolling the other one, and he sees* **Ponce**: *he sniffs and then holds it towards him.* **Ponce** *shrugs.* **Busker** *throws it to him after a moment.* **Ponce** *moves too slowly and the cigarette falls to the ground. And* **Busker** *begins rolling a third for himself.*

Lady (*grins*) Just as well it isni raining.

Ponce (*retrieving it*) Mind you, if it was raining it wouldnt be so bloody cold.

Lady Tch. (*Generally.*) I dont think it's that bad.

Busker *nods in agreement.*

Ponce Christ, I think it's freezing, really freezing! (*Blows into cupped hand.*)

Lady Hh! You must be cold blooded!

Ponce (*seriously*) Naw, I'm no, I'm just . . . (*Stops when he sees* **Lady**

*smiling, and recognises a joke has been made at his expense, though he
is unaware of what it was, but he grins nevertheless.)* **Busker** *has now
finished the cigarette and brings out the matches.* **Ponce** *and* **Lady**
come for a light. **Busker** *lights his own firstly, then* **Lady**, *and then*
Ponce *in a slightly offhand way.* **Ponce** *manages to get the light
without having to inhale and as soon as possible he sticks it out of
sight, unseen by the others.*

Lady *(pause, and generally)* Bloody Birmingham, I cant be bothered
with it.

Busker Not like it then love?

Lady *(sighs)* I wish I could go home.

Ponce You're not the only one. *(Directly.)* How long you been here?

Lady Aw come on, stop asking me all these questions.

Ponce Oh sorry, sorry . . . *(Ironically.)*

Lady Dont mention it. *(Turning from him.)*

Ponce *(nods to himself. Strolls downstage, hands in pockets, whistling
quietly, tunelessly. He dodges slightly to avoid a 'pedestrian')* Sorry
john.

Lady *(gazes after the 'pedestrian', then to* **Busker***)* You going to sing?

Busker Nah.

Lady How no?

Busker *(sighs)* Ah! Just not right love, just not right. *(Shrugs.)*

Lady Och! *(Smiles and shakes head, swivels, twirling hand aloft,
sings:)*

> I'll be with you
> In apple blossom time

(And continues next couple of lines.)

Both **Ponce** *and* **Busker** *are grinning. She is momentarily off-guard.
She breathes deeply, stops moving.)*

Lady Mamma cara . . . *(Shakes head, eyes closed.)*

Busker *becomes preoccupied with his guitar.*

Ponce *(watches the two of them for a time, then strolls forward)* Heh
yous, I'll sing.

Lady *and* **Busker** *look at him.*

Ponce Naw, honest. (*Shrugs.*) I'll give it a buzz.

Busker (*chuckles*) That fucking 'Swiss Maid' jock!

Ponce Naw, honest. I'll sing that one 'Kelly'.

Busker 'Kelly' . . .

Ponce D'you no know it?

Busker (*begins picking the tune immediately and sings the first line*) Kelly and I meet secretly.

Lady (*laughs*) Aw 'Kelly'!

Ponce (*grins*) Aye.

Lady Tch, I've no heard that yin for ages.

Ponce *sniffs self-consciously.*

Lady Good on ye!

Busker *stands smiling.*

Ponce (*a bit unsure now, to* **Busker**, *after a moment's silence*) What will I just sing it bare or what?

Busker No no – no mate. You just kick off, I'll come on in, I'll pick it up.

Lady *smiles from one to the other.*

Ponce (*pause. Watches a 'pedestrian' pass by, and to* **Busker**) So what do I just start then?

Busker (*shrugs*) Might as well jock.

Ponce Alright. (*Nods, purses lips. He unbuttons his jacket and rearranges his shirt collar, tugs the sleeves of his jacket down a bit and turns a little, to be facing side on to the audience, clears his throat, embarrassed, but begins confidently enough, and* **Busker** *follows him in on it*:)

> Kelly and I meet secretly
> We stay out all night
> When we're in each other's arms
> We know it isnt right
> We are so in love
> But he loves you too

(*And continues almost – but not quite – to the straight conclusion.*)
Ponce *sings and* **Busker** *plays as well as each can under the*

circumstances. There is no parody, no sense of irony whatsoever. **Lady**
*enjoys the performance and occasionally gives an encouraging clap to
the rhythm, but the rhythm isnt that good so she never continues it
long. When it has ended* **Busker** *gives* **Ponce** *a nod.* **Ponce** *shrugs and
sniffs, but he knows his performance was adequate.*

Lady No but it was really good.

Ponce Ah!

Lady Seriously but, it was. (*To* **Busker**.) Wasnt it?

Busker Yeh, yeh, it was alright, yeh. (*Footers with guitar keys.*)

Lady (*to* **Ponce**) See!

Ponce (*shrugs*) Ah well, I suppose right enough I've been singing it
for years I mean, I know all the words; it always sounds okay when
you know the words. (*Shrugs.*) No think so?

Lady Yeh, probably. (*Matter-of-fact.*)

Ponce (*shrugs*) You get away with murder.

Lady (*smiles suddenly*) My mammy was a good singer. She knew
them all. All the songs. She knew them.

Ponce *nodding, waiting for her to continue, but she enters a reverie
instead. She sighs, turns from him: she puts cigarette into her mouth
and puffs, puffs strenuously.*

Lady Bloody thing's gone out again! (*To* **Busker**.) How in the name
are you supposed to smoke these bloody things!

Ponce (*calls*) It's a pair of bellows for lungs ye need!

Busker *smiles briefly, preoccupied with his guitar.*

Lady (*to* **Ponce**) Naw but I'm being serious . . . ?

Ponce I dont know. Ask him!

Lady I did. He just didnt want to tell me! Is he in the huff?

Ponce *laughs abruptly.*

Busker (*mild irritation, but smiles*) It's not that love it's only – I'm
supposed to be working you know . . . (*Walks upstage to peer at the
clock on the high building opposite.*)

Ponce (*squints there also*) What time is it?

Busker (*steps back a pace*) Ten after I think.

Lady What!

Both look at her.

Lady (*subdued disappointment*) You mean ten past? (*Peering immediately at clock.*)

Busker Yeh . . .

Lady *closes eyes.*

Ponce What's up like? You got something on?

Busker (*pause*) Alright love . . . ?

Ponce Okay?

Lady (*eyes open now*) Aye, okay . . . (*Smiles. Looks at the pair and turns away.*) What's the bloody difference anyway . . . (*Glances back at* **Busker**.) Come on, give us a song.

Busker *smiles.*

Ponce Come on man give the lady a song! (*Conspiratorial nod to* **Busker** *who shrugs, and* **Ponce** *walks to* **Lady**.) Heh what was that yin you were singing a wee while ago? Ye mind?

Lady (*closes her eyes, holding her hands out to him and starts to sing*) Red red wine . . .

(*And continues on.*)

Ponce *smiling, delighted by her, and eventually he reaches forward and takes her hands, by the fingertips only, and they begin dancing as she sings.* **Lady** *has allowed it as though oblivious to his presence.*

Busker *watches with a smile at first, then tries to ignore the pair as he becomes more aware of the 'pedestrians', seeing their reactions.* **Lady** *now humming the song where she doesnt know the words and* **Ponce** *has begun humming along with her, they are now holding each other, doing a slow waltz. And* **Busker** *is losing patience. Glances at audience and at 'pedestrians' then strums noisily as he returns to stand in his former centre/upstage position.* **Lady** *and* **Ponce** *stop dancing and glare at him.*

Lady *and* **Ponce** *still hold each other.*

Lady Rude bugger!

Ponce (*nodding agreement, angry*) Aye.

Lady Isnt he! Rude bugger . . . (*Leaves* **Ponce** *and faces* **Busker**.)

Ponce (*with her*) Aye you you want to fucking relax man know what I'm talking about, you want to fucking relax, eh! (*Very irritated.*) Moaning bastard . . .

Lady *nods.*

Ponce Christ almighty did ye ever take a look at your face! Eh ya fucking moaning bastard eh! What's up with you at all, fucking moaning-faced bastard!

Busker (*abrupt turn to confront them,* **Ponce** *especially*) What! What did you say! Ya wee fucking bastard ye what did ye say? Eh? What did you call me! Fucking . . . (*Speechless with rage. And his accent has become Glaswegian.*) Wee fucking . . . I'm sick of it, sick of it, just fucking sick it, the pair of yous I'm fucking sick of ye!

Other pair watch. **Ponce** *astonished,* **Lady** *less so.*

Busker Yous fucking on and on yous fucking go, on and on and on yous fucking go, and I'm fucking here, I'm fucking here, having to stand and watch yous, trying to earn my fucking wage man I'm trying to earn my fucking wage . . . ! I'm working. Know what I mean I'm working, I'm fucking working! Ye understand? Eh? Ye fucking understand? Work! Fucking work! (*He continues standing glaring at the pair, but they are more taken aback than anything, and not too cowed by the onslaught.*)

Lady (*quietly*) There is something up with you.

Busker *glares at her.*

Lady Naw, no kidding ye.

Busker There's nothing up with me!

Ponce You're from Glasgow.

Busker So what ya wee cunt ye!

Ponce Might've fucking known!

Busker What might ye've fucking known!

Ponce *just stands shaking his head, glances to* **Lady** *and gives a snort.* **Lady** *shakes her head in agreement.* **Busker** *stares at them for a moment.*

Busker See yous dont know. Yous just dont know. Ah! Fucking stroll on! (*Stops and sighs.*) Christ. (*Shakes his head.*) Listen, I'm here trying to earn, right? I'm trying to earn, I'm trying to get a few quid, I mean this is my living. (*Indicates guitar which he slaps a little fiercely.*) I'm a busker, I'm a fucking busker. I get paid dough for playing some music. That's it. That's what I get fucking paid for, for playing a bit of music. Okay? I'm no here for a fucking party, know what I mean!

Ponce (*shrugs, smiles wryly*) No problem.

Busker Aye, no fucking problem.

Pair gaze at each other.

Lady Hang on a wee minute you. (*To* **Busker**.) I want to say something.

Busker (*slowly, sarcastic*) Do you?

Lady (*up to the sarcasm*) Yes, do ye mind?

Busker I dont mind – fucking free country.

Ponce Aye!

Busker *glances at him.*

Lady (*stares at* **Busker**) I dont think you're a real busker, no a real one.

Busker Eh . . . ?

Lady You're no.

Busker (*disgust*) Christ almighty.

Ponce Tell us something then, how come ye lay on the Cockney accent?

Busker *still affected by* **Lady**'s *last comment.*

Ponce Eh? Know what I'm talking about, I mean what do ye do it for?

Busker *looks at him.*

Ponce (*shrugs*) I want to know.

Busker Do ye.

Ponce Aye.

Busker Aye well I'll fucking tell ye then it's because of ponces like you.

Ponce What!

Busker You, ya fucking ponce ye! You and cunts like ye! Everywhere I go I seem to bump into yous. Eh? How d'you think I left London? (*Half addressing* **Lady** *now.*) I used to have this fucking brilliant pitch man down Bayswater. No kidding ye, fucking brilliant. Aw christ . . . No use talking. Too much. Just too much. There's no use talking. (*Others watch him.* **Busker** *now shakes his head, stares at floor.*)

Lady (*frowns. Pause*) Actually I dont eh . . . naw, sorry, I dont see it, I actually just dont see it, you at Bayswater, I dont see it, being honest about it, I just dont see it, you at Bayswater.

Busker What ye talking about?

Lady I just canni see it, you, at Bayswater.

Busker I dont even know what you're talking about! Me at Bayswater. *At* Bayswater. I mean what does it fucking mean!

Lady Just you at Bayswater, I canni see it. (*To* **Ponce**.) Can you?

Ponce Naw.

Busker I dont even know what you're talking about – at Bayswater for fuck sake it's just a fucking place.

Ponce You know what the lady's talking about.

Busker I dont fucking know what she's talking about.

Ponce Aye ye do, ye know fine well, she means you're no big time enough.

Busker (*puzzled*) What?

Lady Naw it's no that, it's no quite that, that wasni what I was meaning, it's just . . . (*Friendly smile at* **Busker**.) I'm no sure, I just canni see it.

Busker (*shrugs*) It's just a fucking place same as here.

Ponce Uch away!

Busker It's just a fucking place!

Ponce Ah!

Busker *puzzled frown.* **Ponce** *gives a knowing smile.*

Busker What's up with you at all?

Ponce *continues smiling, shakes head.*

Busker Aye well I'll tell ye something for nothing, at least I'm no a fucking ponce. (*Starts tuning guitar.*)

Lady (*glances at* **Ponce** *eventually*) It's right enough but . . .

Ponce *taken aback.*

Busker Coming round here trying to con me.

Ponce Trying to con ye? I'll tell ye something man, if I hadnt started doing the business you'd still have forty pence lying in that fucking tin. Aye and I'm no kidding ye.

Busker Yeh . . . Hh.

Ponce Telling ye dear see before I turned up he'd forty pence in that tin there – forty pence. Then I done a bit of collecting for him. And I got him a few bob.

Busker Got me a few bob? You'd have got me fucking arrested ya cunt! (*To* **Lady**.) Listen, I had to give him a pound to go away! But then he came back. Greedy.

Ponce It wasnt like that.

Busker Was it no? Well what was it fucking like?

Lady (*after a moment to* **Ponce**) Folk *were* putting in the money when I came; and you wereni doing nothing.

Ponce I'm no denying that. All I'm saying is that with me here he was making more – that's all, that's all I'm saying.

Busker (*brief laugh*) Is that right! Heh, listen, listen a minute, I dont want to disillusion you or nothing . . . (*Puts his hand into his jeans' pocket and brings out a bulging handkerchief and also shakes coins in the other pocket.*) D'you think I'd fucking leave all the bread lying in that wee tin! Think I'm fucking daft! (*Unfolds handkerchief.*) See! Fifty pence pieces; pound coins!

Lady *laughs.*

Busker See love, you cant just let the money lie there piling up, otherwise the punters'll walk straight past ye. Cause they see it there and they think: Aw wait a minute, this guy's earning more than me!

Lady You're the bloody conman!

Ponce (*aside*) Ponce.

Busker (*seriously*) I play music. I play music. It might no be very good music but I play it anyway. And as a matter of fucking fact I happen to think it's alright. So I'm giving them something for their money – okay!

Lady (*smiles*) Fair enough.

Busker Aye I know it's fair enough man I play alright, I play alright.

Ponce She never said ye didnt.

Busker (*frowns*) Is it no about time you were going along the road there jock!

Ponce (*to* **Lady**) Jock! D'you hear that? Still calling me jock, same as the English. What d'you make of that! Imagine calling your fellow countryman jock! Hh! Christ! I've heard of some crawlers in my time but that takes the fucking biscuit!

Busker (*jerking his thumb at* **Ponce**) What is he stupit or something?

Lady (*pause*) No think he's got a wee point though?

Busker Listen lady I couldnt care less what an idiot like him thinks! (*Sniffs and adjusts his guitar strap over shoulder.*) Far as I'm concerned this is it, this is the work, it's what I do, it's no a fucking game. (*Takes out his pouch and withdraws a ready-made rolled cigarette and sticks it into his mouth, gets the matches out and lights it immediately*.) Aye and this is my pitch; I get it for two hours the day, two hours. So give us a fucking break eh!

Ponce (*has been shaking his head: he points to the cigarette*) Makes ye laugh right enough. He's had ready-mades hid in his pouch all the time, but didni let us know in case we asked for one!

Lady nods, *but vaguely, is now seeming tired.*

Busker What you fucking yapping about now!

Ponce (*shakes his head*) You, with the ready-mades there. You didnt want us to see them just in case.

Busker Just in case! What do you mean just in case! I gave you a fucking fag every time ye asked I mean . . . (*Derisive laugh*) . . . ye dont even smoke, poncing wee bastard!

Ponce What!

Busker You ya wee bastard ye, ye dont even smoke! You must think we're all fucking absolute fucking idiots! (*To* **Lady**.) Did you notice? He doesnt even smoke! But he's been taking my fags all morning. Probably punts them to the old wineys down the park!

Ponce (*shocked*) I do not do that. Honest. I dont. I would never fucking do anything like that. Never. Never in my life. Hand up to God. (*Raises hand aloft.*)

Busker Then how come ye take them?

Ponce (*pause*) What's it got to do with you?

Busker jeers.

Ponce It's got fuck all to do with you what I do!

Busker (*jeering*) Yeh . . .

Ponce (*jerking thumb at him, to* **Lady**) It's fuck all to do with him what I do.

Lady Well, it is his fags you're taking, then selling.

Busker Thanks.

Ponce But I'm no! I'm no selling nothing! (*Turns to* **Busker**:) I never even asked you for a fag man I mean I didni . . . (**Lady** *should convey a lack of attention in this.*) . . . you just kept fucking giving me them I mean what am I supposed to do, throw them away!

Busker Ah!

Pause. **Lady** *rotates her shoulders a little, as though to aid concentration, suppresses a yawn.*

Ponce Naw but you just gave me them man, understand what I'm talking about, you'd have done the same yourself.

Busker No I wouldnt.

Ponce (*to* **Lady**) Listen to the patter! Naw, he wouldnt've took them, he wouldnt take anything, he's straight as a die – that's how he keeps all his dough wrapped in a fucking hankie!

Busker Aye cause if I dont there's cunts like you'll rob me.

Lady (*quietly resigned*) Oh oh.

Ponce What did you say there?

Busker *laughs.*

Ponce What did you say?

Busker You heard fine well what I said.

Ponce (*to* **Lady**) Did he say I'd rob him there!

Lady *shrugs, she glances briefly in the direction of the 'clock'.*

Ponce Hey, did he say I'd rob him?

Lady It's nothing to do with me what he said . . . (*Glances after a 'pedestrian'.*)

Ponce Aw I see, thanks very much.

Lady (*gazes at him for a moment*) You're awful silly. Ye know that? Awful silly . . . (*Yawns suddenly and covers her mouth with her right hand. Glances sideways, sighs.*) I wish there was someplace to sit down . . . (*Shivers.*)

Ponce *frowns, he looks about.* **Busker** *is now giving his attention to* *the guitar again, and he begins strumming. And* **Lady** *strolls a couple of paces.*

Music: The guitar piece begun by **Busker** *fades into tape of the same.* **Lady** *massages the small of her back, a grimace from her, a sense of pain suppressed. And lights out.*

Act Three

Lights: the males are kneeling by **Lady** *who has fainted.* **Busker** *is the more knowledgeably attentive.*

Ponce (*after a moment*) You sure she's okay?

Busker *grunts, examining her, laying the palm of his hand on her brow, the guitar twisted round to his back.*

Ponce Eh?

Busker *doesnt respond.*

Ponce Ye sure?

Busker (*quietly*) Yeh . . .

Ponce *makes to touch her.*

Busker Dont touch her!

Ponce I wasnt going to . . . (*Rises, continues watching, crouching with his hands on his knees.*)

Lady *groans.*

Busker Alright love?

Ponce Ye okay dear?

Lady (*further movement and a groan as she raises herself onto her elbows, lies back down, then suddenly starts up and grasps* **Busker**'s *wrist*) What is it! What is it!

Busker (*pulling clear*) Heh! (*Tugging her hand.*)

Lady (*still gripping his wrist*) What is it? (*Releases her grip.*)

Busker *Mixed relief/amusement. Massages his wrist, grins at* 'pedestrian'.

Ponce (*pats her shoulder*) You're okay hen, you're okay.

Lady *gazes at him, raises herself into a sitting position.*

Ponce Aye, you'll feel it in the morning!

Lady (*rubbing back of her head*) I bloody feel it the now.

Ponce You're alright but, you just fainted.

Lady (*frowns from* **Ponce** *to* **Busker**) I did not.

Ponce (*grins*) You did.

Busker You did love. (*Also grins, snaps fingers.*) Out like a light!

Ponce Honest. One minute you're standing the next you're bang, out. Lucky the way ye fell too, might've broke your nose or something. A pal of mine done that once, fainted – landed right on his nose and broke it. (*Glances at* **Busker** *who nods.*) Cracked the fucking bone man.

Lady *groans. Not really listening to* **Ponce**. **Busker** *now stands, adjusting his guitar strap etc.* **Lady** *suddenly notices 'pedestrian' and puts a hand to her face.*

Lady Oh God, that's really embarrassing.

Ponce What?

Lady (*mumbling to herself*) Embarrassing, oh God, so embarrassing.

Ponce Dont be daft.

Busker (*quietly*) What d'you mean love?

Lady *now covering her face with both hands.*

Ponce (*goes to her*) Heh you're okay hen, you're okay . . .

Lady Oh God.

Busker (*a step towards her*) Hey love. (*Touches her shoulder.*)

Ponce You just fainted.

Lady All the folk . . .

Ponce (*frowning*) Ach!

Lady They all seen me.

Busker Aw come on.

Ponce Nobody was looking.

Busker Aye, nobody was looking.

Ponce Honest.

Lady Ye sure? (*Glances about.*) Oh God they are, they are, they are so, they're staring . . . (*Quietly.*) . . . they're staring at me.

Both men glance sideways.

Busker You're alright love you're fine . . . just get up. (*Hand to assist her.*)

Ponce (*also assists*) Upsa daisy.

Busker People canni help looking.

Ponce You'd be the same yourself!

Lady *stands shakily.*

Ponce Ye would. (*Grins at her, then walks downstage, calling to audience.*) Roll up roll up! See the fainting woman! Falls on her face and bangs her head! Falls on her face and bangs her head! Roll up! (*Hand cupped to mouth.*) Roll up roll up!

Lady *and* **Busker** *stand smiling,* **Lady** *with less certainty.*

Ponce (*winks at her and walks round downstage calling*) Fifty pee a short look two quid a long yin! Roll up roll up and see the fainting woman, she falls on her face and bangs her head! (*Pause; smiles, hands into pockets, gazing at the other two.*)

Busker *now returns to his stance, brings out his tobacco pouch.*

Ponce (*frowns suddenly aside at a 'pedestrian', mutters*) What're you fucking looking at!

Busker *takes out a ready-made, offers it to* **Lady.**

Lady No, thanks.

Busker Sure?

Lady (*distracted*) No the now . . . (*Examines her clothes while* **Busker** *lights his roll-up.*)

Ponce (*sees* **Lady** *examine her clothes and calls*) Just as well it wasnt raining eh?

Lady *brushing something off the hem of her skirt.*

Ponce (*suddenly*) Heh listen dear, I want you to tell me something, gen up, when did ye last eat?

Lady *looks at him.*

Ponce Naw, serious, when did you last eat?

Lady *shrugs vaguely.*

Ponce I'm being serious.

Lady A wee while ago.

Ponce Exactly. (*To* **Busker.**) See what I mean! (**Busker** *puzzled. And to* **Lady**:) I was saying that to him afore you came.

Lady (*preoccupied*) What . . .

Ponce About eating and that. (*Turns to audience, hands still in pockets, glances back to* **Lady.**)

Lady (*seeing her tights now, and raises her skirt a little*) Aw naw, my tights, I might've bloody known . . . (*Both men stare at her, her skirt still raised: she notices their stare and without making anything of it she drops the hem and mutters:*) Bloody things . . . (*Glances sideways, looking for a place to sit. Sighs uncertainly.*)

Ponce Heh careful! (*Moving to her.*)

Lady I'm alright.

Ponce Ah well you never know. (*Arrives, touches her shoulder.*)

Lady (*shrugging off his hand*) Dont panic.

Ponce Sorry. Sorry, I'm no . . . (*Halts.*)

Lady *looks at him.* **Busker** *also looks on. Pause, then* **Ponce** *continues, a bit flustered:*)

Ponce Naw eh christ I mean you just fainted.

Lady Yeh, well people dont usually faint twice.

Ponce (*still flustered*) What . . .

Lady I'm saying people dont usually faint twice. (*Glances away, re-examining her clothes.*)

Ponce (*sniffs and glances at* **Busker**, *then to her*) I've no heard of that.

Lady *gives him a look.*

Ponce Honest, I havent.

Lady Tch tch tch.

Ponce (*to* **Busker**) You heard of it man?

Busker *shrugs, then strolls to see the 'clock'.*

Ponce (*gazes after a 'pedestrian', murmurs*) Time to go I think . . .

Busker *returns casually to his stance, avoids a 'pedestrian'.* **Ponce** *stares at the legs of this same 'pedestrian' and* **Lady** *sees him do it and he sniffs and looks away. He glances at the tobacco tin on the ground and strolls nearer it, indicates it to* **Busker**:)

Ponce So how ye doing?

Busker Okay.

Ponce Aye good, good, it's nice to get a turn – I thought maybe with all these sales and that . . . (*Shrugs.*)

Busker Brings them out.

Ponce Aye, course. (*Pause.*) They bloody sales but eh! And they all go and spend their dough too, that's what I can never understand. The closing-down sales go up one week then it's the fire-salvage, after that it's fucking January and all hell breaks loose man every cunt goes rushing in, head down, throwing it away, just throwing it away! (*Laughs, shake of the head.*) Jesus christ right enough.

Busker *nods.* **Lady** *doesnt respond.*

Ponce Sometimes you think anybody could con them. Anybody at all. No kidding. It amazes me.

Busker *turns from him and strums a little.*

Lady Ye going to play now?

Busker Nah . . . (*Glances at* **Ponce** *who is now holding his hand out palm upwards, testing for rain.*) Is that the rain?

Ponce Just a spot I think.

Lady (*goes to* **Busker** *with dead roll-up*) Going to light me?

Busker (*brings out pouch*) Want a fresh one?

Lady Och naw, this is fine. Waste not want not.

Busker *strikes match for her.*

Ponce *is aware of being excluded from this interchange. He looks at 'pedestrians' and at one stage does a minor imitation of somebody's walk, but without exaggeration and no one else notices.*

Lady (*to* **Busker**) I'm sorry for all this bother I've caused you.

Busker Ah!

Lady No, I mean it.

Busker Ach forget it.

Lady But you're supposed to be playing your music.

Busker Ah . . . Sometimes I cant be bother anyway, as a matter of fact, if you want to know the truth, I just cant be bothered.

Lady Yeh but you've got to bother. You've got to bother. I'm being serious.

Busker (*nods*) I know you are.

Lady People have to make use of their talent. That's what God gave you it for.

Busker *raises his eyebrows but says nothing.*

Lady Didnt he?

Busker (*pause*) I dont know.

Lady D'you believe in God?

Busker (*shrugs*) Dont know. (*Smiles.*)

Ponce (*downstage from them is nudging something on the ground with his shoe, hands in pockets and lost in thought, sings quietly*) On a mountain in Switzerland yodel odel oh

Lady (*suddenly*) Did you ever play in a band? I'm no being cheeky.

Busker (*sniffs. Pause*) Yeh . . . (*Glances at guitar keys, reaches to touch them.*)

Lady I knew it. (*Smiles.*) I knew it.

Ponce *sidles closer a step or two, now eavesdropping.*

Busker Everybody's played in a band love. (*Accent now half-and-half, returning Cockney.*)

Lady Naw I knew it but, I guessed, really, you're just too good, you're too good.

Busker (*hates hearing this*) Naw naw naw I'm no, I'm no, that's wrong, it's fucking wrong, dont say it, cause it isni true. It isni the way things are. (*Shakes head at her.*) There's plenty of guys better than me love, plenty – much better.

Ponce (*calls*) Know what I think? I think you've got a bloody inferiority complex. Understand what I'm saying? I mean see if I could play the guitar like you! Christ! (*To* **Lady.**) I'd be a fucking millionaire! Excuse the language.

Lady *is listening to this.* **Busker** *snorts and shakes his head.*

Ponce I'm no kidding ye man. I mean you're playing stuff as good as you hear on the telly. Better! Christ, I mean, see if it was me!

Busker You're dreaming.

Ponce That's what you think.

Lady (*to* **Busker**) Still and all . . .

Busker (*generally*) You're dreaming. It's a fantasy shot. (*Directly to* **Lady** *now.*) Yous dont know, you think you do but you dont.

Lady Ah well, it's your business.

Busker (*laughs*) Ah but it's no, it's no my business, it's the bleeding music business. (*Taps himself on the chest.*) If it *was* my business then I would be a millionaire. Yeh (*amused*), me and . . . hh.

Ponce Who.

Busker What?

Ponce You and who?

Busker Nobody.

Ponce I thought you were going to tell us somebody's name there. D'you know any of them like? These ones I mean the famous yins, singers and that.

Busker *smiles.*

Ponce Do you but?

Busker One or two?

Ponce Honest? Who? Come on! Ye going to tell us man, come on!

Busker Barbra Streisand.

Ponce Barbra Streisand!! Do ye?

Busker Naw.

Ponce Tch, ya bastard.

Lady *grins.* **Busker** *laughs.*

Ponce You probably dont know anybody! (*He looks from* **Busker** *to* **Lady** *who shakes her head at him, and he frowns, puzzled.*)

Lady Well it's your own fault. You're always asking these stupid bloody questions.

Ponce (*pause*) He led us on but.

Lady (*slowly*) You're just making excuses . . .

Ponce *stares at her. She sighs, shakes her head slightly, walks a pace.*

Busker (*immediately*) Okay?

Lady *doesnt respond.*

Busker Love . . . ? (*Both he and* **Ponce** *move in readiness to support her.*)

Lady (*shrugging them off in anticipation*) I'm fine, I'm fine.

Ponce Naw but you've just fainted, you must need a seat or something I mean, christ . . . (*Takes her by the elbow.*)

Lady (*shouts*) Stop touching me! You're always bloody touching me. Stop it. Just bloody stop it!

Pause.

Ponce *puts his hand to his forehead: he cannot cope with this.*

Busker He didnt mean it love. He was just trying to help.

Lady I know he was just trying to bloody help. (*Hand to her brow, walks a couple of paces.*)

Ponce If ye want a chair . . . If ye want a chair . . . Do ye want a chair? I can get ye one, if ye want one, I mean . . . (**Lady** *nods without looking at him. He glances at* **Busker**.) Cause that wee cafe round the corner, the woman that owns it, she's a friend of mine – I go in there quite a lot. (*Frowns.*) I mean you'll probably know her as well man, she's got one of these motor cars with the thingwis, at the back . . . (*Describes something unintelligible with his hands.*) These kind of aluminium or something, these bits.

Busker Yeh.

Ponce (*pause. To* **Lady**) I could get you one from there . . . if you wanted . . . (*Shrugs.*) Maybe you dont but . . . ? A chair I'm talking about.

Lady (*looks at him until he becomes embarrassed, smiles*) Come here.

Ponce (*very hesitant*) Naw . . .

Busker *observing.*

Lady You should take better care of yourself.

Ponce (*less hesitant now*) I do alright.

Lady (*nods. Smiles to herself. Walks downstage to peer across at 'clock', watched by both males, and quietly*) Time I was away . . . (*Turns to them.*) Time I was going.

Ponce I dont think you should, no yet.

Busker (*nods*) He's right love I mean eh you're better waiting a minute – maybe going round the cafe or something, for a bite to eat, just to keep you going . . . (*Sniffs and pats his jeans' pocket.*) I've got the dough I mean . . . (*Shrugs.*)

Lady *nods. A brief glance sideways, opening her handbag and looking inside, brings out make-up mirror and touches her eyebrows, primps her lips etc., and afterwards snaps shut the handbag. Other two watch her. When she becomes aware of them she speaks.*

Lady I've got to be going.

Busker *nods.*

Lady It's just I've got to go a message . . . (*Smiles briefly.*) Cheerio.
(*And she exits, the males looking after her once she has gone.*)

Ponce Hh, christ . . . (*Shrugs and steps as though to continue looking
after her, steps again to avoid a 'pedestrian', and eventually turns to
Busker.*) That's funny that . . . (*Half to himself.*)

Busker Is she away then?

Ponce Aye . . .

Busker *nods, starts footering with his guitar, ignoring* **Ponce.**

Ponce *frowns at him, hands into trouser pockets and strolls to the side,
and pauses, glancing back at* **Busker** *who is still preoccupied with the
guitar. And now* **Busker** *begins strumming a blues quietly.* **Ponce**
continues staring at him. The lights fade on **Ponce,** *leaving* **Busker**
alone for several seconds, strumming quietly.

Lights out.

End

IN THE NIGHT

In the Night first appeared at Battersea Arts Centre, London, in March 1987, directed by Jonathan Pope; parts were played by Peter Granger Taylor, Pat Wymark, Wanda Toubas, Kay Adshead and James Castle. The production bore little resemblance to the play I had written. I blame myself as much as anyone for what was essentially a breakdown in communication. Later in the year I directed the play as a Roughcast Production at the Edinburgh Festival Fringe Society; cast was as follows:

Woman	Lilian Cattigan
Man	R. W. Hawrish
First inter	Derek Mcluckie
Second inter	Andrea Hart
Third inter	Stewart Ennis

Music by Alan Tall
Stage managed by Pierre Turton and Ashley Forbes
Photographs by Brian Curley
Administered by Sylvia Anderson

Cast

Man	Late twenties/early thirties
Woman	A year or so older
First inter	Twenty-five to thirty years old, male
Second inter	Late twenties/early thirties, female
Third inter	Thirty-five to forty years old, male

Notes on direction

Throughout the script there are precise directions on movement and
non-verbal responses but the actors should not feel constrained by
these; they can use them as guides to character and to pace. The
accent of each character must be the same. Although the regional
accent used on this occasion is Glaswegian any regional placing where
English is the standard form is possible: the only rider here is that the
RP 'voice' of British authority is excluded at all costs, and that there
should be no class distinguishing features between the five characters.

Scene	A very sparse room.
Time	Around dawn on a summer's morning.
Music	A pervasive presence quietly as background.
Props	A single mattress. A medium, rectangular table. Two large blankets. Two wooden kitchen chairs. One note pad and a pen. One flask of hot tea. Three paper cups. A small rubbish bin. A packet of cigarettes.
Lighting	To be discussed.

Act One

Music has begun prior to lights.

Man *and* **Woman** *lie side by side on the single mattress, covered by the two large blankets. They appear to be sleeping.* **Man** *lies on his back while* **Woman** *is on her side, facing away from him, upstage.*

Ten second pause.

Man (*clearly and with relish*) Their officials burst into the flat at 3.25 a.m. that dry summer's morning, to find him sound asleep beside a woman of pleasing aspect . . . (*Sighs, then chuckles.*)

First Inter *now appears from rear shadows, slowly, staring to both sides of the room, paying no heed to the couple.*

Man (*clasps his hands behind his head. He speaks more loudly than before, a slight nervousness but does not hesitate*) Their officials burst into the flat at 3.25 a.m.; a summer's morning, dry, and they found him sound asleep beside a woman of pleasing aspect. (*Raises his head to peer at* **First Inter**.)

First Inter *pauses. He ignores* **Man**. *He circles the area methodically, gazing sideways now and again. He arrives downstage.*

Man (*glances at* **Woman** *who has yet to move position*) Their officials, they burst into the flat, it was dawn, just after it. (*Looks at* **First Inter** *then lies back down, pulls blankets to his chin. He stares at the ceiling, eyelids parted widely.*)

First Inter (*turns to* **Man**, *folds his arms, nonchalantly*) Did they?

Man *gives no indication of having heard.*

First Inter So they burst into your flat did they! (*Smiles.*) Waal!

Man (*after a pause he raises himself onto his elbows, looks at* **First Inter**) Did you say something there?

First Inter *chuckles, unfolds arms, hands into his pockets.*

Man What do you mean 'waal'?

First Inter (*not smiling now*) You obviously think you're something special.

Man What?

First Inter (*smiles*) A woman of pleasing aspect. Do you truly believe there's something remarkable about that?

Man *frowns.*

First Inter Eh? Something amazing? Something wildly astonishing? (*Steps a couple of paces towards the mattress.*) Sound asleep beside a woman of pleasing aspect! (*Shakes head, smiling.*)

Man Some folk would find it interesting.

First Inter Would they?

Man *clears throat as though to speak, but doesnt.*

First Inter You convinced about that? Are you?

Man Can I smoke?

First Inter (*perfunctorily*) No. (*Continues walking.*) You live in a wee fantasy world, dont you?

Man *lies down again, clasps his hands behind his head. He clears his throat once more, but says nothing.*

First Inter Did she have any clothes on?

Man What?

First Inter Did she have any clothes on?

Man You talking to me?

First Inter (*chuckles. He resumes walking, whistling in a vague, tuneless manner: then he stops abruptly and shakes his head*) Did he?

Man (*stares at him*) What . . . ?

Woman (*still lying on her side facing upstage*) He did. Yes. He had his clothes on.

Man *glances over his shoulder at her.*

First Inter Ahh, I see.

Woman *turns to lie on her back and stares at* **First Inter.**

Man *leans and whispers to her: inaudible to anyone but her.* **Woman** *nods in reply to him.*

First Inter (*sharply*) What was that? (*Pause. Eh? What did you say?*

Woman You'll never know.

First Inter *stares at her.*

Man (*smiles very briefly to* **Woman** *before replying to* **First Inter**) My fantasies are my fantasies.

First Inter Yeh well they're not mine, that's for sure. (*Resumes walking*.)

Woman *and* **Man** *exchange looks, unnoticed by* **First Inter**.

Man (*to* **First Inter**) A lot of folk live their lives dreaming about such events.

First Inter Do they?

Man Yeh.

First Inter (*nods*) Good. Because I dont.

Woman (*raises herself up, holding blankets to cover her breasts*) No, you dont.

First Inter That's correct, yeh, I dont.

Woman Maybe that's your problem.

First Inter (*shakes head*) It's not. (*Now to* **Man**.) So, these officials you were rambling on about, as a matter of interest, just as a matter of interest – whose did you say they were again?

Man (*smiles at* **Woman** *before replying to* **First Inter**) Ha ha.

Woman (*annoyed, to* **First Inter**) For god sake!

First Inter For god sake! That's a good one that!

Woman *frowns, then glances at* **Man**.

First Inter (*to* **Man**) No, just as a matter of interest, the ones that came bursting into the flat . . . whose did you say they were again?

Man Surprise surprise, I didnt.

First Inter You didnt. Mmhh. I see.

Man Yeh, that's right, as you know fine well.

First Inter (*sharply, scowling*) And was it her?

Man (*guiltily*) What . . . ?

First Inter (*contemptuous*) You heard.

Woman *puzzled; looks at* **Man**.

First Inter Yeh. (*Nods.*) This is really smelly you know. (*To* **Woman**.) His fantasies I mean, so-called.

Man Aw come on.

First Inter Come on nothing.

Woman (*after a pause*) Would you mind very much if we put some clothes on?

First Inter (*staring at her. Grunts. Resumes walking, then he glances at her*) Is it you then . . . ? This – what did he call it – woman of pleasing aspect, is it you?

Woman (*wearily*) My god.

Man (*to her*) It's alright.

First Inter (*commands*) Quiet. Shut up.

Man *silenced; downcast.* **Woman** *bows her head.*

First Inter (*to* **Woman**) You see dear, I'm trying to unravel some sort of modicum of factual matter from all the garbage he talks, your man there – because that's what he talks, garbage.

Man How come I cant get a smoke?

First Inter Because I say so.

Woman You're so childish, you really are.

First Inter Aw, am I, is that a fact.

Woman Yeh, it is, you're so (*shaking her head*) immature.

First Inter (*sudden grin*) Aye well it's no me that lies in bed giving vent to a bunch of erotic fantasies.

Man Tch.

First Inter Nope. It's not me.

Man (*to* **Woman**) Enough said.

First Inter Enough said, yeh.

Woman He was talking to me.

First Inter *stares at her. Then he strolls upstage, pauses by the window, gazes out, absently.*

Man *significant look to* **Woman** *who nods.*

First Inter (*turns from window. He strolls forwards, and to* **Man**) I dont like you very much do you know that. You're a fart. That's what you are, a fart.

Man *stares straight ahead.*

First Inter (*to* **Woman**) A fart. (*Jerks thumb at* **Man**.) Your man there. (*Pauses.*) I've got the position of power dear, that's how come I can say these things.

Woman *just stares at him.*

First Inter (*hand to heart*) Oh you're frightening me, you're frightening me!

Man *mutters under his breath, something like 'ya dirty bastard' but it must be inaudible to all except* **Woman** *who does not respond.*

First Inter (*sarcastic*) Pardon? (*Five second pause.*) Were you saying something there?

Man *shakes head.*

Noises off: a bumping.

First Inter (*he has heard but pays no attention*) Okay, because I thought you were and that wouldnt be fine at all, it just wouldnt be fine at all. Now (*folding arms*) where were we . . . The officials burst into the flat did they . . . Mmhh. Yes. Good. (*Turns and strolls to door and opens it.*)

Enter **Second** *and* **Third Inter**, *walking as though their timing has been so perfect they havent had to break stride. They come forward, gazing at* **Man** *and* **Woman** *on the mattress, but with no especial interest.*

First Inter (*indicating* **Man**) He's got great and unimaginable fantasies this yin. Ask him.

Second Inter No thanks.

Third Inter (*stares at* **Man** *and* **Woman**) No time, unfortunately, though I can go a good fantasy now and then. (*Directly to* **First Inter**.) So, where've you got and what's been happening?'

Second Inter (*to* **First**) Was it her?

First Of course.

Second (*looks at* **Man**) And him?

First Yeh.

Second Mm. (*Nods.*)

Third (*strolls downstage then turns abruptly to* **Woman** *and* **Man**) Okay: up!

Woman *and* **Man** *lift blankets and arise. They are naked. They stare ahead, standing where they are.*

Third Okay okay, you've made your point. (*Bored.*)

First *grabs the blankets and hands one each to* **Woman** *and* **Man** *who* *drape them round themselves. Then* **First** *looks to* **Second**, *his hands clasped behind his back.*

Second (*bored*) They're just being humorous.

First They've been like that from the start.

Second Ah. (*Nods.*)

Third (*frowns at the* **Couple**) Are you trying to humiliate us? Is that what it is?

Pause.

Second *smiles and strolls downstage, peers off.*

Man We asked for our clothes earlier on, but he wouldnt allow it.

Third Wouldnt allow it . . . (*To* **Man**.) Is that a fact?

First I said no. (*Hands still clasped behind his back.*)

Third Oh.

Second (*turns to face* **First**) I trust you had a reason?

First I did.

Second (*pause. And to* **Third**) What do you say?

Third I say yes. Full agreement.

Second (*slowly*) Fine. (*Strolls.*)

Third (*to* **First**) So?

First (*shrugs*) He's been going on about being in bed with a woman.

Third Nothing more?

First No really – apart from the description, the way he described her, the woman, as being of pleasing aspect. He said she was a woman of pleasing aspect.

Third (*nods and gazes at* **Woman**. **Second** *also gazes at her.* **Third** *now walks to* **Woman** *but addresses* **Man**) Do you like your wee fantasies son? I say that because you seem to.

Pause.

First *smiles at* **Third**, *shaking his head, his hands still clasped behind his back.*

Third (*to* **Man**) Did you hear me talking to you there?

Man (*clears throat*) Aye, but I didnt think it was a question.

Third You didnt think it was a question . . . (*Nods. To* **Woman**.) What about you? Do you like him having these wee fantasies?

Second Maybe they're about her!

First They're not.

Second No, I didnt think they would be.

Woman (*wearily*) Oh god.

Third *turns to* **First**, *frowning as though puzzled.* **First** *nods, grinning.*

Second (*to* **Woman**) You're an atheist, arent you?

Woman (*after a moment*) Is that a crime now as well?

Second *stares at her, then strolls to the chair at the table, sits down and gazes out the window.*

Third Of course. Yes.

First She knew that already.

Third I know she did.

First I would think probably they're both atheists.

Third Both atheists. Yeh. In other words, they dont believe in God.

First Aye, that's right.

Third Mmm.

First Though maybe he's just kidding on he's one: to impress her.

Third *chuckles.*

First Because guys like him do that, they go about trying to impress people, about their self-sufficiency etcetera. As if anybody gives a shite.

Second *glances at him.* **First** *nods in response to her.*

Third Boring people. Boring people. (*Pause. Frowns. He looks at the couple.*) I wonder whether they know their rear-end from their elbow.

Third *strolls downstage and turns abruptly as though to roar at* **Man**, *but says nothing.* **First** *laughs for a moment.* **Third** *now turns to face off, clasps hands behind his back. Couple watch him. Meanwhile* **Second** *takes a notebook from her pocket and leafs through the pages.*

Pause.

Third (*sighs. Glances at* **First**) Do you know what, sometimes I honestly crave getting back onto dayshift. I do. It's a genuine craving. Just to get myself away from certain types of disturbance.

Second *glances curiously at* **Third.**

Third (*to* **First**) Certain forms of it. The kind that happen at night. Or only seem to happen at night. Do you know what I'm saying?

First (*grins. Looks at him, awaiting further comment. None comes. Pause*) You talking about sex? About sexual matters?

Third Well aye, yes, I suppose. Things that happen at night. Generally though, I'm speaking generally, in general terms.

First (*nods. Then suddenly*) Will I tell you how they were when I first appeared?

Third *makes no sign, so* **First** *glances at* **Second** *and* **Second** *nods.*

First (*continues, addressing both colleagues with some animation*) Side by side, right. The pair of them. On the mattress there, the bed; and you would have thought they were asleep, the way they were lying, not moving, not moving hardly at all, just lying there, side by side. Then I hears this voice. And it's him (*jerks thumb at* **Man**) talking away as if it was a picture he was watching, an erotic one. Maybe even as if it was going to be a wet dream or something.

Third Well well. Hh!

First *chuckles.* **Woman** *glances at* **Man** *who seems downcast and* **Second** *turns another page in her notebook as though having lost interest.*

Third (*frowns. He strolls to* **Woman** *and gazes at her*) See when you say you're an atheist, what exactly do you mean?

Woman (*stares straight ahead*) Can I have some clothes?

Third In a minute. (*Circles couple and stops by* **Woman** *again.*)

Second (*to* **Woman**, *but without glancing at her*) You were asked a question.

Man She knows she was asked a question.

First *and* **Third** *look at each other with exaggerated surprise, then amusement.*

First (*to colleagues*) He's really tough but isnt he!

Second (*smiles*) No intimidation though.

First I wasnt about to. (*Amused.*)

Third But I was, I was. (*Unsmiling.*)

Second *smiles. Returns her attention to notebook.*

Third (*gazing at couple*) Not even a little bit? Eh? Just a little bit?

Second *smiles; gazes out window.*

First (*looks at* **Man** *while addressing* **Third**) I'll tell you what I think, that's if you were to ask me, and I was being honest about it, the whole thing, if I was being honest about the whole thing, it's smelly. Smelly. Not only that, it's irritating.

Third You find it irritating too, eh?

First I do, aye.

Woman Oh god.

Third *grins. Jerks thumb in direction of* **Woman.**

First These two but, they dont; they dont find it irritating. At least I dont think they do.

Third It's a pity.

First It is a pity. Mind you, sex and smelliness and things like that, they all go the gether.

Third *does not smile as* **First** *expected.* **Third** *only nods, turns away, and strolls.*

First (*calls after him*) No think so?

Third *smiles vaguely.*

Second (*to* **First**) You're being silly!

First Sorry . . . (*But doesnt appear sorry.*)

Second *continues to gaze at him for a time, then returns attention to notebook.*

Third (*clasping hands behind his back*) Aye, indeed. (*Apropos of nothing. Then to* **First**.) Basics eh! Basics.

First Of course.

Man *shifts stance. Moves his shoulders as if they had been stiffening.*

First (*to* **Third**, jerking thumb at **Man**) Your man there, he's getting impatient. I think he wants to be on the move.

Third (*with relish*) On the move. Do you think so?

First (*staring at* **Man**) I do, aye.

Third Maybe he requires the lavvy!

First Maybe. I doubt it but.

Third You doubt it. Mmm. I'll ask him anyway. Hey eh . . . eh . . . Do you require the lavvy?

Man *stares straight ahead. Both* **Woman** *and* **Second** *also gaze at* **Man.**

Third Right enough you know he could be wetting himself. That's what happens with heroes a lot of the time, the condition of incontinence – ever notice that? (*Pause. Strolls round* **Man**, *giving an exaggerated sniff at his backside. Smiles at* **First**, *and gives another sniff.*)

First (*also smiles then notices* **Second** *glancing at her wristwatch, and he nods and addresses her*) But it was funny. They hadnt heard me at first, they didnt know I was there. It was like I just suddenly *appeared*! And then there was this voice. (*Indicates* **Man**.) Rambling on in a kind of weirdish fantasy tone, if you could call it that. Also, when he knew I was here, your man, he started injecting a bit of sarcasm into the timbre, the tone, the way he was saying it.

Third Sarcasm? (*Glances at* **Second** *who is listening to* **First** *attentively*.)

First Well, it sounded like sarcasm to me.

Third Did it?

First It did, aye.

Third Mm. What else?

First Yeh fair enough what else but still I mean do you no find it funny how come they can achieve it? This yin for example. (*Indicates* **Man**.) And he *was* wetting himself just like you said, he really was.

Third *raises his eyebrows.*

Second (*frowns*) I wish you'd find a more informal method of description.

First What?

Second Something less rigorous. (*Shakes head. Now peers out window.*) It's rather offputting. Silly in fact. (*Glances at* **First** *again.*) If that's all you can derive from it, your method.

First (*quiet defiance*) Sorry. (*Glances to* **Third** *then back to* **Second**.)

Second (*frowns*) Anything further?

First Well eh another thing I was immediately thinking, considering just, I mean, to do with the relationship, the relationship they had: if it was permanent; if it had been finalised in some sense; were they married or what?

Second (*nods*) They're not married.

First They're not married. (*Nods.*)

Man *turns and slowly whispers to* **Woman** *who smiles.*

Third (*commands*) Quiet!

First I've caught them whispering before, when they thought I wasnt listening, when I wasnt looking. Maybe he's braver than we think!

Third Though there again mind you there's a difference between bravery and bravado.

First (*notices* **Second** *look across and calls to her*) I caught them whispering before.

Second And what about exchanging things. Did you see any of that? Did you for instance catch him in the act of giving her something – an object of some sort?

First No. Not at all. They were naked.

Second *continues looking at him.*

First They're naked. (*Glances quickly at* **Third**.)

Second They could've hidden something in the blankets, within the folds.

First They didnt.

Second Did you check? (*Pause, then to* **Third**.) Did you check?

Third I didnt, no.

Second *nods.*

Third I didnt think it necessary.

First I didnt either.

Second Fine. If you're sure.

First (*nods and continues to* **Third**) So, when I was standing, just as I was standing there . . .

Third (*interrupting*) Irrelevancies, you're coming out with irrelevancies.

First What?

Third *shrugs.*

First But it's got to be done.

Third *shrugs and turns away.* **First** *frowns.*

Second (*slight impatience*) Just let's get on.

First (*shrugs*) It doesnt matter anyhow. It's only I thought each wee nuance might be of possible significance, that it might be of possible significance, each wee nuance. Or at least relevant, I thought it would be at least relevant.

Second Yes?

First Although fair enough because I see it as relevant, obviously that doesnt entail its being relevant, not its actually being relevant, eh . . . (*Tails off, aware of* **Second** *watching him.*)

Second Doesnt it?

First (*puzzled: adopts a 'thinking' posture*) Eh . . .

Second (*gazes patiently at him, then glances at* **Third** *before continuing to* **First**) You simply cannot hope to get them all without either going in front or going behind. It is just not possible. In other words, if you hope to procure them all you must already be scoring through others. And I mean all the time, including those you assume to be irrelevant. Underline that. (*Glances at* **Third** *then back to* **First**.) And dont worry about it. You must simply set them out, putting forward the ones you recall at the given moment. Then you stick to it, you simply stick to it. You have to disregard failure. Completely. Decisively. If you do not do that then you cannot *hope* to achieve an objective. Truly. (*Glances again at* **Third** *before continuing to* **First**.) There is not anything that is more certain.

Pause.

First *nods.* **Second** *now shifts her seated position, gazes out window.* **First** *clears throat, peers at* **Woman** *and* **Man**, *then makes a hesitant movement.*

Third (*to couple*) Yous pair, you're beginning to cause no little dissent amongst my friends and colleagues.

Woman We're sorry.

Third No you're not. That's the thing you arent, sorry. You're not sorry. You're not sorry at all. There's a central problem.

First It's no really a problem. What it is, they think because they're atheists and anti-establishment that they're already in front to begin with. (*Strides a couple of paces, his annoyance seems genuine.*)

Man *moves his hand slowly out from his blanket and touches the* **Woman**'s *shoulder.*

First (*immediately*) Look! Touching her!

Third Was he touching her there!

First Right in front of your bloody eyes he was touching her! Just where you were standing!

Third *gazes at couple.* **First** *comes directly in front of* **Man** *and stares right into his face.* **Second** *closes notebook, unnoticed by anyone, leaves it on the table and rises, strolls downstage.*

First (*shakes his head to her, jerks thumb at* **Man**) See this yin!

Second He actually touched her while you were both standing there beside him?

First Unbelievable! The insolence but, know what I mean, the actual insolence! A person like this!

Third Aye, you said it, a person, because he's no a man! If he was a man, a real man . . . Eh! Can you imagine a genuine real man being in a plight like this!

First You're right. You're dead right.

Third They're no even married. If he was a real man they'd be married.

Second They dont believe in marriage.

Third What!

First Honest?

Second (*walks to* **Woman**) They dont. (*To* **Woman**:) Tell them.

Woman There's nothing to tell.

Second There's everything to tell. You dont believe in marriage, and you dont believe in children. And you dont believe in the family, nor in its sanctity.

Pause.

First But what about the Royal Family? And its sanctity? Do they believe in that? I mean surely they believe in that?

Second Of course not.

First For heaven sake!

Third That's really terrible. (*Matter-of-factly.*)

First Do they believe in nothing at all? What about our other institutions, surely they believe in them, our other institutions!

Second They dont. They believe in nothing. Nothing. They dont believe in anything. Not a thing. Not a single solitary thing.

Woman Not even that we're standing here being threatened by you.

Man *reaches to touch her for a moment.*

First Heh you, you and the lady here, a question . . .

Man *stares ahead.*

Third Somebody's talking to you.

Man But he hasnt asked me anything yet, so I dont have to answer.

Third Of course you do.

Man But it's daft.

Pause.

Third What?

First What was it he said?

Third I'm no too actually sure. Indeed, I think he said it was daft. Or I was daft. Or was it you? (*Strolls behind* **Man** *and makes as though to give him a rabbit punch in the small of the back, witnessed only by* **First** *who grins.*)

Second Mmmm . . . (*Absently.*)

Third (*to* **First**) You know something, I'm beginning to get sick of them, these two. (*Paces about, containing energy.*) Before I was just bored and a wee bit irritated. But now, now – now I'm getting totally browned off. And aye, I've got to admit it, the first actual stirrings of anger, of that possibility.

Second *and* **First** *both nod.*

Man (*clears throat*) We didnt ask you to come here.

Third Oh goody.

Second (*to* **Woman**) You're being impressed.

Woman Yes. Thanks for advising me of it.

Second Not at all, it's alright – it's part of what I do well. (*Turning from* **Woman**.) And does your husband know about this? (*Pause.*) Does he?

Woman Does who?

First Her kind doesnt have husbands.

Third *puzzled frown at* **First**, *then strolls to sit at the table, looks out window then stares at the notebook, and lifts it.*

Second (*to* **Woman**) It isnt easy asking you those questions.

Woman *stares ahead.*

Second (*glances at* **Third**) Thanks . . .

Third *rises and takes notebook to* **Second** *and she puts it into her pocket.*

First (*to* **Third**) That bravado you were speaking about earlier, mind? What was it you were saying about it?

Woman Can we please have some clothes?

Third Note the please!

Second *smiles.*

First Aye but it was still done while I was talking. She interrupted me. She interrupted me! (*Very angry.*) It really makes you . . . (*Stops himself from going any further. And still containing his rage, he addresses* **Woman**:) Do you always interrupt people?

Second *and* **Third** *watch him closely.* **Man** *and* **Woman** *stare ahead.*

Pause.

Second You were being asked a question.

Woman (*after a moment*) It was rhetorical.

First It wasnt.

Woman (*after a moment*) It was.

Man *moves as though to go closer to* **Woman** *but doesnt.*

Second As a matter of interest, it was not rhetorical.

First Of course it wasnt, it was straight, a straight question.

Third A straight question.

Woman Oh god.

Man How come we cant get our clothes?

Second I dont know. You tell me.

Man Because you wont let us.

Second Ho! (*Shakes head, turns from them: gazes off.*)

Man Give us our clothes.

First (*to* **Third**) Listen to the fart!

Man Yes.

First (*pause*) What? (*Glances at* **Third**.)

Third Dont look at me.

Second (*to* **First**) Did we bring the flask?

First Eh . . . (*Puzzled.*)

Third It's outside.

Pause.

First (*glances from* **Second** *to* **Third**) I'll get it. (*Goes to door.*)

Second Fine . . . (*Walks slowly towards couple.*)

First *stops by door and gazes back at the others.* **Second** *looks at him and he exits.* **Third** *strolls to* **Second** *and he whispers something to her and* **Second** *nods, but makes it plain that she doesnt want to continue the private interchange.*

Third (*strolls on, encircling couple, then halts abruptly*) Do you regard yourselves as ordinary British citizens? (*Laughs to* **Second**.) I've got a feeling that they're Irish, d'you know that. Indeed. (*To* **Man**.) Am I right am I wrong? Irish? Is that it? You want to be ruled by the Pope? Eh? Is that your Defender of the Faith? The Pope? His Holiness the Pope? (*Shakes head.*) Well well well eh, imagine wanting to get ruled by the Pope! Tch tch tch! And you a good atheist too! That's what I cant understand, the thing that is incomprehensible to me.

Woman *bored sigh.*

Third (*stares at her. Calls to* **Second**) They're dominated by contradiction. Folk like this. Not think so?

Second I do, yes. I'm in full agreement.

Third I mean it must be difficult even walking down the road: one foot going this way and the other going the other! (*Chuckles.*)

Second *smiles.* **First** *now enters with flask of tea and three paper cups. He pauses and gazes at* **Second** *and* **Third** *in a surreptitious manner, then continues to set the things on the table.*

Third (*calls to him*) Hey, this pair here, I've just been finding out, they want to get ruled by the Pope!

First What did you say?

Third (*jerks thumb at* **Woman**) According to this yin anyway!

First Maybe they're no atheists after all!

Third Exactly what we were thinking. Mind you, if they dont believe in the Royal Family and they dont believe in God, and now here they are wanting to be ruled by the Pope – or is it not wanting to be ruled by the Pope . . . ! You hardly know where you are!

Second You're being silly.

Third Silly . . . ?

Second *turns away.* **Third** *stands there a moment, then walks to table where* **First** *is unscrewing top of flask.* **Third** *sits.*

Second (*to* **First**) Give it a minute yet.

First (*stops unscrewing top*) Yeh . . . (*Sniffs.*) I only thought . . .

Second *looks away from him.* **First** *glances at* **Third** *who is peering out the window.* **First** *hesitates then strolls upstage behind the couple in a slow but methodical fashion, hands clasped behind his back.* **Man** *shifts position, aware of* **First** *somewhere behind him.*

Woman Can I touch his naked shoulders?

First *taken aback, then he glares at* **Woman.**

Second (*sighs*) It's just to annoy us. Minor humiliations.

Third *stares at* **Second.**

First (*looks from* **Woman** *to* **Man,** *and addresses* **Second**) Do you think she really likes him?

Second *shrugs.*

First I dont see how it's possible.

Couple edge closer together.

The **Three Inters** *all see it happen.* **Third** *leaves the table and comes forward.* **First** *glances at* **Second** *as though for instruction.*

Second (*raises her right hand calmly*) Let matters rest here a moment, and things of importance be indicated.

First *and* **Third** *both nod.*

First About what we've established?

Second (*glances at him*) About what has *been* established, yes.

Third *smiles.*

Pause.

First Well . . . (*Stares at couple who now are shoulder to shoulder.*) . . . certain items, indicators; pointers in a sense, I suppose – guides we could call them, to character and personality . . .

Second (*wearily*) Mmmm.

First For example . . . (*Pause. He notices* **Third** *peering at him.*) . . . certain things I would regard as eh, well, I suppose for instance even the atheism, just, the atheism, that lack of belief in God as Almighty, an inviolable supremity. And eh the Royal Family of course, no belief in that – our Heads of State too. Plus as well you've got ordinary family life, its sanctity. (*Shrugs.*) Actual authority, you've got that. (*Frowns.*) As vested in ourselves. They dont give it a fitting respect, I wouldnt say so . . . It seems to me they really just flout it, the sarcasm and eh . . . When they know it too I mean it's no as if they're in ignorance I mean if they were in ignorance, a genuine real ignorance, if it was that, but it's not, because they're in full awareness, they've got a full awareness, they bloody know. They bloody know fine well! (*Glances at* **Second** *and shakes his head significantly.*) So when they know too I mean . . . it's eh . . . eh . . . I mean it's no as if they're in ignorance.

Second *nods.*

First Eh . . . (*Hesitant smile.*) Mmm . . . (*Adopts a 'thinking' posture.*) Not his fantasies . . . (*To* **Second**.) D'you mean his fantasies? Is it his fantasies?

Second (*waits a moment*) Are you making a statement?

First *just looks at her.*

Second You are stating something.

First Eh . . .

Second Either it is yes or it is no. (*Pause.*) It has to be one thing or it has to be the other. (*Suddenly to* **Third**.) Do you agree?

Third Eh . . .

Second Do you agree?

Third (*frowns*) Well eh not exactly. Not exactly.

Second (*raises eyebrows. Then to* **First**) Proceed.

First (*a pace forward and back again*) Their sarcasm I would say I mean, mainly I suppose. That sense of it coming out in different –

also isolated – forms; it comes out in isolated forms, as a series of incidents of authority flouted. Even that last 'naked shoulders' carry on. (*Jerks thumb at* **Woman**.) The way she did that, how she just said it. Then as well of course you've got it right the way back to when they just stood up and were nude, their bodies, them being naked like that, without covering it up, their nudity, just standing for that split second, without doing it.

Second So, then, you have an inference?

First Oh well it's precise that we're here.

Second You would say so.

First Yeh. (*Looks to* **Third** *and back to* **Second**.) Yeh.

Third *smiles and turns away.* **First** *frowns at him.*

Second Nothing more?

First Nothing more . . .

Second Nothing further?

First *frowns.*

Second No? (*She turns to* **Third**.) Do you think there is?

Third Yeh.

First Well aye, right enough, obviously I mean there must be, I know that, of course, but I'm just eh I'm just eh, not up to thinking it all out, not at this exact moment, the way everything is, the situation . . . (*Shrugs, then change of mood*.) It's as if . . . as if . . .

Second Pardon? As if?

First As if . . . (*Frowns*.) I dont know really . . . It's just no conducive or something – the atmosphere, the entire atmosphere, of this place. (*Looks about him and shivers*.) It's not got the proper sort of atmosphere, something in the air, something just . . . (*Tails off and stares at the floor*.)

Third *glances round at everything, as though checking* **First**'s *claim.*

Second Mmm . . .

First *makes hesitant movement.*

Second No, I'm not disputing your claim, I'm not, not necessarily.

First *stares at floor.*

Second We'll let it pass for the present at any rate. (*To* **Third**.) What do you say?

Third Me?

Second On the question of potential indicators, matters arising, from what has been established.

Third (*frowns*) About everything?

Second Yes.

Third (*glances from* **Woman** *to* **Man**) In terms of probability you mean?

Second If you like.

Third (*nods*) I take it you mean in front of everybody?

Second Not if it embarrasses you. (*Smiles.*)

Third What?

Second Would it embarrass you? Are you easily embarrassed?

Third No.

Second Are you sure? (*Smiles, but not unfriendly.*)

Third I am sure, yes, indeed.

Second I just wondered. Some people do tend to be. They tend toward it.

Third I'm not one of them.

Second Fine. (*Studies* **Third**.)

Third *drops gaze from her, and stares at his shoes.*

Second Alright?

Third (*looks at her*) Yes.

Second (*shrugs*) Sorry.

Third There's nothing to be sorry about.

Second That's good. You see what worries me, what occasionally worries me . . . (*Absently walks a pace or two.*)

First Does it concern minor humiliations?

Second (*glances at him*) Yes . . . but I'm probably just thinking aloud. What was that early derivation of his? (*Indicates* **Man**.) The description of the woman, can you remember?

First He referred to her as a woman of pleasing aspect.

Third (*chuckles*) A wee male fantasy.

Second Is it?

Third (*pause. Shrugs*) Very likely.

Second (*sudden impatience. She glances at her wristwatch and at the window, then briskly*) We must process things more readily. (*Glances at colleagues, at the couple.*) I shall state very briefly what I dislike about them and why I feel they are to be punished rightly. And I'm aware you can find it peculiar. It is just that they are not us. (*Puzzled shake of the head: frowns at couple.*) There is something distinctly unwholesome about it, about both it and the circumstances surrounding it. Something that makes me uneasy. A measure of unhealthiness; a thing that is unhealthy, that makes me want to shudder. (*But she must not shudder here.*)

First Yeh. (*Vigorously.*)

Third Aye . . . (*Whispering.*) I feel it, I feel it.

Second *shuts eyelids firmly, head raised slightly.*

First *steps across to* **Second** *and whispers into her ear.* **Second** *smiles, opens her eyes.*

Third *frowns at his colleagues.* **First** *just looks at him.* **Woman** *and* **Man** *turn to see what is happening.*

First (*at couple*) Heh!

Third (*commands*) Face the front!

Couple do so at once.

Second (*mild surprise*) So brazen!

First So nosy!

Third *shakes head.*

First (*moves toward the couple, clenching his right fist, grinning at* **Third**) It would be nice to just . . . (*Makes as though to strike the couple.*)

Woman *and* **Man** *stare ahead, unaware of what is being described.*

Second *turns from them.*

Man Can I smoke?

Third Of course – if you keep your fags in that bloody blanket!

First *laughs.*

Third (*to* **Second**) They just will not learn. They wont. They wont learn. I doubt if they ever will.

Second *smiles.*

First (*also smiling*) Can I be sexist a minute? (*His colleagues gaze at him. He stops smiling.*) Naw eh . . . It's eh . . .

Second No, go on.

First (*pause. Then he looks at her and looks away*) It's eh . . . silly, a bit silly. (*Looks at* **Second**, *sniffs.*)

Second (*pause*) It's this sort of thing I detest. I have never been able to fathom just why it occurs. Yet it always does. Always. And at the same time always, too, it remains beyond the scope of prediction. (*Still addressing colleagues.*) Do you know that general sensation of being in a war against an army composed entirely of spies, of covert agencies, where every last individual looks exactly like yourself?

Colleagues gaze at her expectantly.

Second You make it all too plain. (*Turns and walks to couple, addressing colleagues:*) In the most important sense possible you know, those who are closest to you are often the very ones arraigned in opposition.

First (*clears throat*) I didnt mean it the way it sounded.

Second (*puzzled glance at him. Closes and opens her eyes*) Certain factors often seem peripheral. (*To* **Woman**.) Do you ever feel that?

Woman (*directly*) You're a fascist. Nothing else is of any real account. (*Shakes her head.*)

Second You're wrong, as matter of principle. I'm not a fascist.

Woman Yes you are.

Second I'm not.

Woman (*pause*) Yes you are.

Second (*to colleagues*) She calls me a fascist!

Woman You are.

Second (*smiles*) I take it you mean all three of us? Or is it only myself? Am I the lucky one?

Woman *stares ahead.* **Man**'s *hand appears from blanket, he touches her wrist for a moment.* **Third** *smiles.*

Second Only me I think. She presumes such a term must annoy me. (*Smiles at* **Woman**.) Has it never occurred to you that terms like these are an irrelevance. Your derivations are of no signal interest whatsoever. None. People such as yourself seem to believe their very utterance alone is enough to send a body into apoplectic frenzy. (*Pause.*) You're naive.

Woman *glances sharply at* **Second** *who smiles, steps back and looks at her colleagues.*

Second Take note: how annoyed she's become. Angry even. All because I've described her as naive! It's extraordinary. Extraordinary.

Colleagues smile then **Second** *stops smiling and frowns at* **Woman.**

Man Are we to be given our clothes?

Second How gallant. He's allowing her breathing space.

Third Maybe he is courageous after all!

Second Is she?

Third Yeh.

Second (*to* **First**) Think so?

First (*nods*) Aye.

Second Is it important? (**First** *puzzled.*) Do you care one way or the other? You see I'm rather uncertain about what you think.

First I just dont like them, that's what I think. The pair of them, I just dont like it, them.

Second And you want it made public?

First I dont care.

Second *turns from him and strolls to sit at table.* **First** *stares after her, then gazes at couple with evident dislike. But couple dont notice.* **Third** *moves off, as though losing interest. And* **First** *now goes to table, sits and begins examining his pockets, as though looking for something.* **Second** *has taken out her notebook and resumes reading from it.*

Man (*blinks and chuckles absently*) It's these newspaper articles in front of my eyes . . . or even . . . (*Chuckles. And all turn to watch him,* **Woman** *quietly amused.* **Man** *continues:*) . . . as if I'm taking part in a picture, or a story. And there's somebody reading out the narrative bits. And they're saying about me how it was when I did the thing, the whatever it was, the hasty deed, the bold action, the existential fucking mover – the whatever it was! Aw christ! (*Chuckling.*) You hear this voice, the narrator, talking about me as if I was the real character, and there's this vision, an image, I'm creeping along . . . (*makes the overhead movement of a one-armed swimmer doing the freestyle, one hand still clutching the blanket*)

. . . and it's at the side of these great big bushes, gigantic ones, a tremendous thick undergrowth. And there's spotlight beams away over and they're continually swivelling, swivelling, swivelling, maybe going to pick me out for fuck sake but no, on I run, quietly and steadily christ I'm going to get away with it . . . (*His chuckle here is a bit sly and he glances from side to side furtively, as if looking for a danger.*)

Third is in **Man***'s line of vision at this point but although they stare at each other* **Man** *doesnt appear to see him.* **Third** *frowns at his colleagues.* **First** *rises from the table but remains standing where he is. Then* **Second** *also rises, shaking her head.* **Woman** *now stares to the front.*

Second (*walking slowly to behind couple*) No, I dont believe it. I dont believe it.

Third A wee con perhaps?

First Or another fantasy! He loves these fantasies! Batman and Robin! Maybe he saved up Yankee comics when he was a boy? Heh you! Did you?

Third (*laughs briefly, then to* **Woman**) He really enjoys the fantasy routine eh!

Woman (*clears throat*) He's no the only one.

Third What?

Second It's alright, she's referring to me . . .

Third *frowns.* **Woman** *stands rigidly.* **Man** *leans his shoulder to her. And* **Second** *speaks calmly:*

Second Shift them apart, now.

Both **First** *and* **Third** *come to do so, they escort each separately to opposite sides of the stage, neither of the couple offering the slightest resistance.*

Man Can I have a fag please?

Third I'll tell you something for nothing son, if we say aye then you better start worrying.

First *laughs abruptly.*

Second (*to* **First**) Tea.

First Eh, yeh, I'll get it.

Second Thank you.

First *strolls to table.* Second *takes notebook from her pocket, glances through the pages: now she nods to* Third *who nods in reply, and he turns, begins whistling tunelessly – more of a loud breath than a whistling sound. Eventually* Man *shifts his stance.*

Third Keep your eyes to the front, son!

Man *moves again.*

Third Come on!

First (*while unscrewing and perhaps pouring a cupful of tea*) Do as you're told!

And Third *frowns at him, irritated.*

Woman How come you call him son so much?

Third (*pause*) Because he's younger than me.

Woman (*sarcastic grunt*) Yeh, and he always will be.

Third (*pause*) You'll make me angry in a minute!

Woman Good.

Third (*deadly earnest*) You will actually.

Woman (*pause*) Good.

First *is now seated sipping tea; he takes a copy of* The Guardian *from his pocket, and reads it, without unfolding it fully.*

Man How come we cant get our clothes?

Third (*smiles*) She prefers you the way you are.

Man (*smiling*) I know.

Third (*stops smiling. He glances at colleagues at table but neither seems to have heard*) Dont do it too often son. It doesnt pay. I mean that, it doesnt.

Second *glances up from her notebook and across at* Third *who now approaches* Woman.)

Third And how long yous been together then?

Woman Not long enough.

Third (*nods matter-of-factly*) And you're quite happy to admit to that are you? I mean that you both are living together and having a full sexual relationship, even though yous arent married? You admit it?

Woman Admit it! I'm proud of it – I've been trying to have a full sexual relationship with him for years!

Man *chuckles.* **Second** *leans to whisper something to* **First**, *but it doesnt seem related to what is happening with* **Third.**

Third You are both subversive elements, you are radical left-wing communists. (*Couple smile.*) Loonies . . . ! (*Couple smile.*) Dont be humorous about it!

Woman I apologise.

Third You dont mean it. So dont bother even saying it. (*Strolls to* **Man**, *then roundabout both him and* **Woman**, *and he calls to colleagues:*) Sarcasm's beginning to become them!

First *smiles.* **Second** *does not respond, just sips at her tea, gazing out the window.*

Third (*calls to* **Second**) Would it be absolutely invalid to lose one's temper?

Second *smiles.* **First** *laughs quietly.*

Third (*jerks thumb at* **Woman**) Honest, I'm beginning to think she's a transvestite! Maybe they're both a pair of bloody homos!

Woman (*wearily*) Oh god.

Second *A vague smile to* **Third**, *then stares out window.*

Man Surely we can get our clothes?

Third (*smiles to* **First**) Their clothes!

Woman Can we sit down?

Third Sit down! (*To* **First**:) Hear that! Sit down! (*Roars:*) They'll be wanting to go bloody back to bed next! You see . . . (*Controlling himself.*) You see . . . with all this long list of grievances yous've both got, what I want to know – just for my own benefit – what I'm wanting to know – how come yous dont emigrate! Eh? D'you understand what I'm saying, how come yous dont bloody emigrate? If you hate Great Britain so much as all that then surely yous must want to leave, eh! To go and stay somewhere else, eh!

(*Shrugs, calmly.*) Because that's what I would do if it was me; indeed, it seems obvious, the obvious course: if you need a direction – that's what I'm talking about, a direction, if that's what you need, you both need.

Pause.

Second (*yawns quietly, closes her notebook and calls to* **Third**) Just leave them . . .

Third *hesitates.*

Second Come and have your tea.

Third (*smiles*) Aye, but what I dont understand about them . . . (*Smiles again. Glances at* **Man** *then at* **Woman**, *both of whom stare rigidly to the front.* **Third** *now saunters, turns abruptly and shouts.*) You are a pair of bloody loonies! Lunatics! Do you know that? Are you aware of it? Has no one ever told you? None of your best bloody friends! That you're a pair of bloody lunatics! Yous are a pair of bloody lunatics!

Couple flinch under this but continue to cope. Colleagues are gazing across as **Third** *clasps his hands behind his back and strides a few paces, and calls across.*

Third Arent they! Damn pair of lunatics! They should get locked up!

First *nods.* **Second** *almost does so, continues gazing at him.*

Third Look at them! (*Steps closer, to wag his right forefinger into* **Woman***'s face.*) The smugness! How smug they are! The way they just stand there looking the way they do. Trying so hard not to lose their self composure! (**Woman** *doesnt flinch.*) As if they think they're fooling you! Look at them! (*Strides to* **Man** *and stares into his face.* **Man** *succeeds in remaining calm.*) The insolence! See the insolence! Eh? Plus that assumption, there's always that assumption: that we're of substandard intelligence! Do you know what I mean? Like it's a presupposition! It's underpinning everything! Every damn thing! (*Peers at colleagues.*) That, is what I cannot go, I just cannot go. And I'm no afraid to admit it. Because it damn well bloody sickens me. My stomach. Right in my stomach, like it's a worm gnawing away. As if they're fooling you! Their little games of fantasy. Then that superiority; all the time that superiority, underpinning everything.

Man *now flinches under* **Third***'s scrutiny. And* **Third** *walks to* **Woman**, *jerking his thumb back at* **Man**.

Third Look at him, your man there, he's shitting himself! Hh! Courageous! Hh! Boring! Boring! That's what I'd say: bloody boring! (*He strides to stare into* **Man***'s face again. And again* **Man** *flinches.* **Third** *shakes his head contemptuously.*) Nobody here would even piss on you son, dont worry about that!

Third *has now calmed down.* **Second** *has her arms folded and she gazes downstage.* **First** *is glancing at* The Guardian. **Man** *and*

Woman *stand as rigidly as before.* **Second** *lifts teacup, then reaches for the flask as though to give herself a refill.* **Third** *gazes at her.*

Freeze these positions for some fifteen seconds, then lights and music extinguished simultaneously.

Act Two

Music begins two minutes prior to lights.

Couple stand in exactly the same positions as at the end of Act 1. **First** *is standing, his* Guardian *back out of sight in his pocket. At the table* **Third** *sits where* **First** *was earlier, his jacket is off and draped over the back of the chair; he is holding cup, still with a small amount of tea to drink.* **Second** *sits where she was before.*

Pause.

First (*begins speaking as though in mid-flight*) Death does have its good points though, fair enough, all that stuff you no longer have to do. There again but, all that stuff might just happen to include the details you like in life and wouldnt mind doing for a while yet, given the opportunity. I'm thinking of basic matters.

Third Basic matters?

First (*gestures at window*) Seeing the sunrise for example. (*Sudden grin.*) Okay, sex. (*Serious again.*) Taking your weans down to the seaside, sandcastles and the rest of it, paddling ponds. Christmas. Seeing in the New Year with your friends and family. Plus all the other social oblique domestic activities you have to get involved in every now and then.

Third Mmm . . . (*Shrugs.*)

First (*glances from him to* **Second** *who nods vaguely, gazes out window*) Yous obviously dont agree.

First Eh well, it's not exactly that, not exactly, it's more . . . I dont know . . . (*Slowly sips from cup.*)

Man *unnoticed by anyone raises and holds his left hand aloft.*

Third I think, indeed, if I'm to be honest about it, I'm just no as positive as you.

First (*frowns, smiles*) It's no to do with that.

Third Mmm.

First It's not. I mean I'm no all that positive myself. (*Glances at* **Second** *but she doesnt respond.*)

Third Oh I wouldnt be too sure. Even making statements about things you like. I would suggest that that in itself is positive, it's being positive, it's a positive action.

First But it's no! Heaven sake, you can know what you like without being positive about it, without making positive statements about it, them, the things you like in life. A lot of people know what they like in life and they wouldnt be ashamed of admitting it. Surely you're no going to turn round and tell me they all have to start being classified as positive? (*Pause. Smiles.*) Or are you? (*Stops smiling.*)

Third (*smiles*) Maybe not. But still and all, I've got to say it, these statements you're always making, they're decisions. And if they're decisions . . . (*Shrugs.*)

First (*after a moment*) I'm no so sure. I mean I dont think I would be happy describing them as decisions. Honest. When you're saying that you're saying a heck of a lot, and it strikes me that to make that sort of leap, from there to someplace else . . . I mean . . . well . . .

Third So how would you describe them then?

First Not like that.

Man *Still unnoticed, takes his left hand down.*

Third Would you not?

First No. (*Pause.*) No, I wouldn't.

Third (*raises eyebrows*) Well I would if it was me.

Second (*turning from window*) So would I.

First *frowns at them both.*

Man (*raises hand aloft again*) Can I please go to the toilet?

No one responds.

Second (*to colleagues*) What else can they be?

First I just dont think I could ever have described them as that, decisions.

Third But surely! It's decisions about what you like, the significant things, these aspects you appreciate; sunrise – seeing the dawning of a new day you're talking about, and the sex and the rest of it. Fine. Smashing. Indeed. I mean it, every word. In fact I have to admit it, I envy you as well, I do. Honest, and I'm not at all kidding. You're able to arrive at this that and the next stage; showing preference, stating demands. These events you wish to see happening, how progress is to be shaped, then to take place . . .

Man *lowers his hand, still unnoticed.*

Third (*smiles from* **First** *to* **Second**) Because I cant. I just cant. I've never been able to. Not even as a wean, back when I was a wee boy rushing here there and everywhere. This sounds funny, but take strolls with your parents in the evening sunshine: I've always had a daft regard for that. Always. Even now I've got my own family, my own wee boy and wee girl, I want to take them out just the same. (*Chuckles.*) Whether they want to or no. And yet, if I am being honest about it, I dont even know, I mean I am yet to be convinced – because I can never work it out properly – that it's a thing I can talk about. Or rather, perhaps, a thing that actually *can* be talked about. D'you know what I'm saying?

Pause.

Third *rises from chair, strolls sidestage. Both colleagues gaze after him.* **Third** *gazes vacantly at* **Woman**.

First My own thoughts, right – I think you're best just diving straight in and shouting to yourself: This is great! This is really great! Astonishingly great! This is what I really like and must want to keep on doing. At all costs!

Second Ho! (*Amused. Shakes her head.*)

First (*doesnt smile*) Aye, okay, fair enough, you're smiling, but if I could manage it I'd be well away!

Second Of course. So would everybody.

First Aye but . . .

Second There's no aye buts. There arent any. If what you say was true and could be managed then we shouldnt be requiring solutions all the time.

First *Puzzled frown to* **Third**.

Second We shouldnt. There just wouldnt be any problems you see. None at all. There would be none whatsoever. They would've evaporated, they would've disappeared into thin air.

First Eh . . . (*Smiles.*) I think that's what I was trying to say.

Second Do you?

First Yeh, I think, definitely.

Second (*glances at window then back to* **First**) I'm afraid you may still be realising things far too simply, in far too *acritical* a fashion.

Third (*to* **First**) I dont think it's possible to think the way you do at all! (*Grins, but not unkindly.*)

First Aw come on!

Third (*strolls to table to swallow last remains of tea from his paper cup*) I dont.

First *stares at him.*

Second (*to* **First**) Well you know when one finally accepts a few basic truths – for example, that people are dying of starvation the wide world over, every day of the week, every week of the year, every minute of the day, second of the hour; one two three . . . four five six . . .

Third (*also to* **First**) Yeh you see you cant do it. Not really. It just doesnt become a possibility. It ceases to exist as one. When you know what's going on; in the real world. Out in the real world. When you see what's happening there. Because once you have become aware of certain matters you will always know, always – 'even unto the last days', the bitter end. (*To* **Second**.) Is that correct?

Second (*non-committal*) Mmmm.

First Well what the heck else do you do? For heaven sake! What the heck else is there? I mean you've got to do something, havent you! (*Strides a pace or two.*)

Couple now stand with heads bowed and blankets held tightly, almost as if they are asleep on their feet. **Third** *crumples paper cup noisily, tosses it into waste-bin, puts on his jacket.*

First (*stares at* **Man**, *walks beyond him, stares at him again, then addresses colleagues*) Otherwise you crack up. I would anyhow. I'd take a maddy. I'd go mental. (*To* **Third**.) So would you! So would anybody! (*Doesnt look at* **Second**.) I've seen it happen to folk before. And I'm speaking about good folk. Ones who were strong. They were strong and good. They were brave, and didnt give in easily.

Pause.

Second What's that got to do with anything?

First (*stares at her*) Pardon?

Second (*rising from her chair*) I dont see what that has to do with anything, with anything at all, not really, if you crack up.

First If I crack up . . . ? If I crack up I crack up.

Second *studies him.*

First I'm talking about if I crack up, if you crack up. If you crack up you crack up.

Second Yes?

First You crack up. (*Shrugs.*) Finito. (*Looks away from her.*) Finished. Kaput.

Second (*glances at* **Third**, *then to* **First**) So, fine, for the sake of argument, you've cracked up; so what?

First How do you mean?

Second *Pause. She gestures at* **Third**, *indicating window.* **Third** *goes to window and peers out, eventually returns during next part of dialogue.*

Second (*to* **First**) But it's how you mean, not how I mean.

First Well I mean if you crack up; if you have a breakdown. You're finished. Kaput. Cheerio, you're out the game.

Second Yes I see all that: but so what?

First *stares at her. Then he smiles, adopts a 'thinking' posture, but is ill at ease.*

Second Are you alright?

Third *smiles in the background, shaking his head.*

First (*to* **Third**) What are you shaking your head for?

Third *just smiles, but not unkindly.* **Second** *folds her arms, gazes at her wristwatch.*

First (*to* **Third**) Come on . . . (*And to* **Second**:) If yous dont tell me I'll never know.

Third No it's just, okay, you've reached that fine point where you crack up; and then you do crack up – so you've cracked up. So what? (*Shrugs and glances at* **Second**.)

Second (*after a moment, to* **First**) Dont worry about things unduly.

First I'm not.

Second That's good.

First But I'm not, I'm not worried.

Second (*returns to sit at table*) It can often be a mistake to worry unduly, to take matters too seriously. (*Takes notebook from pocket.*)

First Yeh I know, I mean I do know that.

Second That's good. (*Stares out window, closing notebook.*)

First (*glances from* **Second** *to* **Third**) I think I've missed out somewhere. (*Smiles in direction of couple.*) An implication or something.

Third *raises eyebrows then, hands in pockets, he strolls downstage, whistling tunelessly.*

Second's *attention drawn to something outside window, but only slightly.*

Third (*comes to a halt, stops whistling and sings quietly [tune is irrelevant, a jingle, with stress on 'boozers', 'beaks' and 'Salvation Army'].*)

> We are boozers all
> You can tell it by our beaks
> We're members of the Salvation Army

Third *now continues tuneless whistling, gazing out over audience, hands still in pockets.*

Second *marks something into notebook, another glance at wristwatch.* **First** *staring at his shoes. Couple stand with heads bowed as though sleeping.*

Third (*strolls a pace, calls to* **First**, *indicating couple*) It's good the way they can stand like that for so long, isnt it. Know what I mean? It's as if they get into a trance.

Second (*calls*) They do though! That's precisely the case.

Third Yeh I know but it's as if they're sleeping standing up!

Second Well they are, in a sense: if you were to walk across and poke them somewhere sensitive then you couldnt guarantee a response.

Third But you could predict one, surely?

Second You can predict anything.

Third Well . . . (*Smiles.*)

Second Cant you?

Third Oh aye, aye, yeh. Yes, indeed. (*Shrugs.*) So can anybody.

Second (*looks from him to* **First** – **First** *has been attending to his colleagues' dialogue with interest.* **Second**, *generally*) People frequently take things in too serious a fashion. It can be a wonder to behold. It's larger than life.

Third *and* **First** *exchange glances.*

Second As far as I'm concerned it becomes a sure sign of self-centredness. It's the style of individual activity I regard as sterile. (*Pause.*) It's an abuse. (*Looks away and out window, then studies her wristwatch, and indicates* **Woman**:) What accent did she have?

First Eh, nothing in particular.

Second It wasnt Irish?

First I dont think so.

Third Mind you, it could've been.

Second Think so?

Third Well . . .

First I dont think it was.

Second I must say I dont either.

Sound of jet plane coming into earshot, not as though to drown everything out, but loud enough to have **First** *and* **Third** *almost ducking. Then* **First** *shivers.*

Third Fly so damn low these things!

Second Yeh.

First *walks to window, peers upwards, eventually sits.* **Second** *also looks out but only for a moment, then she leafs through notebook.* **Third** *now acts as if a piece of grit has landed in his eye, but not exaggerated.*

Pause. A real sense of silence for ten seconds.

Man *suddenly raises his head, speaks calmly, clearly; and it galvanises others:* **First** *starts out of his chair and stares at him.* **Woman** *raises her head and stares at him.* **Second** *and* **Third** *also stare. When* **Man** *speaks he addresses audience:*

Man It's this fear of explosions. So absolutely fucking fundamental. It's a fear of explosions. The big bang. In the beginning. Sometimes it's even just sitting in front of the gasfire, the fucking gasfire, just sitting there, you look at it and think: In the name of fuck, it's going to explode! Right in my face! It's going to explode! Christ! Quick! Dive! Run for cover! Quick! Duck! (*Laughs and shakes head.*) But it's only that really, nothing else, I dont think nothing else, just a blank . . . (*Chuckles.*) Well wait a minute, I do, I do think something else . . .

Second (*disbelieving smile*) I dont believe this.

None pay heed to her.

Man It's a picture. I get this picture. Of me. Being shot straight up into the fucking air, with all the debris coming crashing through the wall, bricks and mortar!

Woman *grins, relaxes at last.* **Second** *frowns at her.*

Man (*still chuckling*) I see myself with all my hair standing on end and I'm fucking falling and I'm trying to scramble to catch onto something like a parachute. A big fucking gigantic lump of concrete but – that's all I catch! (*Brief laugh.*) A big fucking gigantic lump of concrete . . .

Woman *laughs quietly at him.*

Man (*turns to her, grins*) Everything flying through the air! All sorts of debris. And I'm thrashing about there, the wee legs going like the clappers!

First (*pause. To* **Second**) He's a bloody conman him so he is.

Couple turn to look at **First.**

Third (*commands*) Face the front!

First (*to colleagues*) Eh? His wee fantasies; all his wee fantasies.

Third Yeh . . . aye.

First *sudden nervous laugh.* **Third** *walks towards* **Man.**

Third You like your wee fantasies son, eh!

Woman (*nervously, but stares ahead*) He's always been like this.

First We can see that!

Third *chuckles into* **Man**'s *face:* **Man** *flinches.*

Third (*to* **Woman**) Have you never considered hospital treatment?

First For the mentally disturbed! (*To* **Third**:) Yeh, maybe she looks after him! (*To* **Woman**:) Are you his doctor?

Woman He's my nurse.

First (*now almost at breaking point, he strides to her, bunching his fist as though to strike her*) It's a surgeon she'll be needing!

Man *cannot see, exhibits anxiety on her behalf.*

Third Face the front you!

First *is coming down from the emotional peak.* **Second** *nods calmly to* *him and he notices, breathing loudly, regularly, rotates his shoulders perhaps, flexing his fingers, then bows his head, eyelids shut.*

Second (*rises, smiling briefly, to* **Woman**) But the idea of hospitals has occurred I take it?

Man *shifts position again.*

Third Face the front!

Second Has it?

Woman (*clears throat*) Do you think it has?

Second I'm asking you.

Others attentive to this.

Woman I hear you.

Second (*pause*) I'm glad that you do.

Woman You make things plain.

Second It's what I'm best at.

Woman (*pause*) And do you expect an answer?

Second (*smiles*) That's an answer.

Woman (*pause*) I thought it would be.

Third (*to* **First**) You know something, I dont even think she's British let alone anything else.

First They're probably immigrants.

Third Yeh, indeed, of Asian or East European extraction. Maybe from Africa, or the West Indies, the Central Americas.

First But they could be Irish, like you said before.

Third Yes, they could be, they could very well be . . . (*Circles* **Man**, *and as he does so calls to* **Woman**:) Eh, excuse me eh . . . Could you tell us how long you've been at the present address?

Woman (*clears throat*) Resident you mean?

Third Just begin at the beginning. This address, how long you been living here, that's all.

Woman Seven months.

Third Ah. Seven months! And you're the breadwinner I take it? (**Woman** *doesnt respond.*) Seven months . . . Mmhh. Did you say seven months?

Man *Swift glance at* **Woman**, *noticed by colleagues.*

Woman About that, yeh.

Third (*hands clasped behind his back, businesslike*) And have the pair of yous been the gether for this entire period of time?

Woman *doesnt respond.*

Third I'm no being nosy. I'm just interested.

Woman Just interested?

Third Yeh. (*Grins.*) Just interested.

Woman (*shakes head*) Right from the very start you've been interested in that. Right from when you first broke in. (*Shakes head.*)

Third (*genuinely puzzled; frowns at* **Second**, *jerking thumb in* **First's** *direction, and to* **Woman**) It's no me, it's him, you're mixing me up with him, it was him that was first in, no me.

First *frowns at* **Third** *who frowns back at him.*

Third She's mixing me up with you.

First (*glares at* **Woman**, *walking towards her*) Heh what is it you're saying? What're you meaning?

Woman *clears throat but says nothing.*

First (*to* **Third**) She's meaning something.

Again **Woman** *clears throat.*

First Eh! I cant hear you! (*To* **Second**:) She's meaning something!

Second *nods, non-committal.*

First (*to* **Woman**) What're you talking about?

Woman (*stares straight ahead*) Right from when you first broke in.

First I never broke in. I never broke in. You must be mixing me up with somebody else. Unless you were dreaming, you must've been dreaming.

Woman I wasnt dreaming.

First You werent dreaming! What do you mean you werent dreaming! You were asleep. You were bloody asleep! Or supposed to be! (*Pause.*) Maybe you werent right enough. Maybe you were awake! Maybe you were just kidding on you were asleep. Is that it?

Others attentive now.

First (*winks at* **Third** *who smiles*) I mean you were supposed to be sleeping soundly, soundly. You were supposed to be sleeping soundly. That's what the man said, soundly sleeping. (*To* **Man:**) Heh you! The lady here, was she no supposed to be sound asleep? (*Laughs at* **Woman:**) You were supposed to be sound asleep!

Woman That's nice.

First (*already stepping across to* **Man**) See that, your cohabitee there, while you were spouting the erotic fantasy, she was awake. She was awake. She wasnt sleeping at all! Hh! Wide awake! And listening, she was wide awake and listening! (*Laughs.*)

Second *gazing at him.*

First (*notices and jerks thumb at couple*) Wide awake and listening! Eavesdropping. She was eavesdropping into it all the time! Listening to every individual word, every telltale individual word! Eh? I wouldnt fancy that! (*To* **Man.**) That'd make me shudder. My cohabitee? Listening in to my erotic sexual fantasies! Oh no, I wouldnt fancy that! I wouldnt fancy that at all!

Woman (*tired*) Not only were they not erotic, they were not sexual. What makes you think they were even fantasy?

First (*sarcastic*) I beg your pardon?

Woman *holds blanket more tightly about herself.*

Second (*bored*) It doesnt matter. (*Strolls to table.*)

First *frowns at* **Third** *who shrugs and looks away.*

Man (*raises arm aloft*) Can I go to the toilet? It's getting to the desperate stages.

Third (*grins*) The desperate stages!

Man I've been needing for a while.

Second *nods at* **Third.**

Third I'll go as well.

Third *and* **First** *go to* **Man,** *taking an arm each, blanket still securely round him. They lead him out through door.*

When door closes lights and music off immediately. Ten second pause.

Then lights and music simultaneously. Sound of cistern refilling. Door opens and the trio return; colleagues on either side of **Man** *as before.*

Second *is standing by* **Woman** *and they are in the middle of a dialogue.*

First and **Third** *also in dialogue. They continue apart until directed otherwise.*

Third Not at all.

First Honest?

Third I'm telling you.

First It's bloody hard to believe.

Third (*whispers*) Well, it's true.

First (*whispers*) Aye but . . .

Third (*whispers*) I'm telling you.

By this time **Man** *is back in position. The dialogue between the two women has gone as follows:*

Second None of you ever do.

Woman Listen to who's talking.

Second You know absolutely nothing about me.

Woman Just that you're a fanatic.

Second As you are.

Woman Of course.

Second Yes, of course.

The three men now listening to their dialogue.

Woman Well then.

Second *smiles.*

Woman (*to* **Man**) This one here, she's always had a secret hankering for the trappings of poverty. Plus, believe it or not, she likes you.

Man (*grins*) What?

Woman It's true; she confided in me when they had you out at the lavvy.

Man Christ!

Woman What she said was, I quite like your man.

Man *laughs briefly. Colleagues frown, glance at* **Second.**

Second (*controlled smile*) Now obviously – and even saying such a thing sounds absurd – the woman is speaking absolute nonsense.

Woman What she said was: I quite like your man.

Second *smiling. Colleagues are uncertain.*

Man (*chuckling*) And what did you say to her?

Woman I told her you were not my man.

Man *laughs quietly, briefly.*

First (*to* **Woman**) Aye you're right he's not your man. He's not anybody's man. I dont even think he's a man at all. Know what I think? I think he's a fart.

Third (*to* **Man**) You are you know. A smelly object who requires to be taught a lesson.

First (*to* **Man**) You do. My colleague's spot on.

Third A lesson of the short and sharp variety.

First *grins.* **Woman** *makes as though to touch* **Man** *but he is far too far away.* **Third** *strolls towards her, hands clasped behind his back.*

Third Indeed. The truth of the matter is, you've been causing a deal of trouble. That dissent! Terrible, really terrible.

Second Do you suppose the two of them wish to bring down the government?

Third I do, aye.

Second It does occur to me you know that they might wish to bring about the complete destruction of our whole way of life. The actual fabric of our entire existence. Do you suppose it's possible?

Third I certainly do.

First It's unbelievable!

Second But is it possible?

First Yeh, now you come to mention it.

Second So we're unanimous. Good. But perhaps we should ask them to confirm or deny the charge.

Third (*after a moment*) You heard!

Second (*to* **First**) Put it to them.

First Do you pair wish to bring down the government, and do you wish to bring about the complete destruction of our whole way of life, the actual fabric of our entire existence?

Woman Of course. (**Man** *laughs.*)

Second (*to* **First**) And ask whether the hostile methods they must flagrantly resort to can be defined as unconstitutional?

First Can the hostile methods you must flagrantly resort to be defined as unconstitutional? (**First** *experiences no difficulty whatsoever in repeating these directives.*)

Woman Obviously.

First (*to* **Man**) What about you?

Man Of course, if she does I do.

First *frowns. His colleagues look at* **Man. Woman** *chuckles.*

Second Ask them if their legs are sore.

Colleagues both laugh briefly.

Second As a matter of interest, I certainly dont think she's Scottish.

Third I told yous before. I think the pair of them are either from Russia or North Pakistan. Maybe even Cuba! No, they're no from Cuba . . . (*Chuckles.*) They're no wearing beards!

First (*laughs*) How do you know! They might be disguised! That could be false faces they're wearing!

Third I never thought of that! (*To* **Second**, *jerks thumb at* **Woman**:) Hey! Can I punch her on the chin to see if she's wearing a beard! Beneath the mask!

Second *smiles.* **Man** *flinches.* **Woman** *bows her head, closes her eyes.* **First** *chuckles.*

Third (*stares seriously at* **Woman**, *addressing* **Second**) Eh? Can I?

Colleagues gaze at **Woman.**

Man *bows head, shoulders hunched. Pause. Then he makes the sound of a fart, a raspberry, but neither loudly nor exaggerated.*

First *frowns at colleagues.* **Second** *smiles slightly. No response from* **Woman.**

Pause.

Third (*generally*) You think you're hearing things at times, dont you!

First You're no kidding!

Third (*to* **Second**) It's as if they're always trying to make fools of us.

Second They are, or pretending to be. (*All* **Three Inters** *gaze at couple, whose heads are bowed.*) They have to do it. There's nothing else for it. It's a facade. But they have to maintain it. Or else everything crumbles. It falls apart. There's a total disintegration. I mean of everything. Welter upon welter of contradiction. One two three, everything goes. (*Suddenly to* **Third**:) You said they were Irish, do you still believe that?

Third Well eh . . . if I'm to be truly honest . . . eh.

Second You're no longer convinced? (*Pause.*) I see.

Third But I knew it was a possibility.

Second A definite one?

Third Indeed. Yes. But I would say now that they most positively arent, they arent, they arent Irish.

Woman (*raises her head a little, wearily*) We arent Irish.

Man *doesnt respond.* **Woman** *bows her head once more.*

First It's that sarcasm, that's what I find so detestable, I mean I just cant go it, that sarcasm. I get so scunnered by it, by this, this kind of . . . (*Stares at* **Man** *and rubs his belly as though feeling nauseous.*)

Third Cheeky bastard. He's a cheeky bastard.

Second (*nods after a moment*) Yeh, he probably is. (*Frowns at* **Woman**.) She isnt though. (*Strolls to stare at her.*)

Woman *keeps her head bowed, but her eyes are open.*

Second She's more . . . I dont know. I'm not a hundred per cent certain what she is.

Third Neither am I.

First (*almost to himself*) It's how come they can be so bloody cheeky . . .

Second (*to colleagues*) No. I have to confess, I'm not a hundred per cent certain. (*To* **Third**.) What would you say? (*Pause.*) Your opinion I mean.

Third My opinion . . . Eh. (*Pause.*) I dont really know. (*Quick glance at* **First** *who looks away, then to* **Second**:) What I feel, in all honesty, sometimes – indeed quite a lot of the time really – is just, that it's better not to enter into things, the last details, that it's better not to enter into every last detail.

Second (*smiles*) What age are you?

Third (*pause*) Thirty-six.

Second Thirty-six. (*Smiles.*) Dont lose it. It's something to stick to. At all costs. (*And to* **First**:) It's important. It really is. (*To both* *colleagues*:) It really is. Not everybody has it. Whatever you do dont lose it. (*To* **First** *suddenly*:) Do you agree?

First Agree . . . ?

Second (*stares at him. Then to* **Third**) Do you agree yourself?

Third Eh. Yes.

Second You're sure? You dont sound confident.

Third I am confident.

Second You are confident?

Third Enough.

Second *continues gazing at him.* **Third** *doesnt flinch.*

Second (*nods*) Good . . .

Second *turns from* **Third**. **Third** *glances at* **First** *who has been watching intently.*

Second (*addresses them both*) We're learning a fair amount. No matter what we may think, we are. All learning takes place through a process akin to revelation. Then comes the straightforward processing. (*Smiles.*) So dont worry. (*Directly to* **Third**.) Dont worry.

Third (*frowns*) I'm not.

Second That's fine.

Second *looks to* **First** *who drops his gaze eventually.* **Second** *now nods to* **Third** *who walks to the window, peers out. Then* **Man** *makes a sudden movement.*

Man What was that! (*Glances right to left, clutching blanket, shivers, seems almost terrified.*)

All stare at him. **Man** *now clutching blanket as though for protection, he is close to cowering.* **Woman** *stretches her hand to him, and her face, for a short span of time, appears set to crumple. But she regains her composure and her hand returns beneath blanket; she stares at floor.* **Man** *peers sideways, now recollecting the present situation; and he looks to* **Woman**:

Woman (*tired smile*) Okay?

Man Aye. Whhoh! Jees . . . (*Total relief now.*) My god! (*Pause.*) That was a fucking beauty that – ho! Christ. Dear oh dear!

Woman *after a moment gazes back to the floor.* **Third** *and* **Second**

exchange glances. **Second** *looks at colleagues then at couple, clears his throat.*

Man (*addresses* **First,** *but only because he happens to be the nearest person*) Tell you something pal, see if I was you, I'd get really sick of that nightshift! What're you permanent? (*Pause.*) Whhoh! Fuck sake, it must be murder! (*Peers roundabout.*) It's in the atmosphere eh! Something! (*Peering slowly around.*) I dont know what it is. Maybe it's just the actual place itself, it makes you fucking shiver so it does. We've spoken about it before.

First (*puzzled irritation*) What? Spoken about what? What you talking about?

Second *looks from* **First** *to* **Third,** *then continues watching* **First** *who has now walked to face* **Man**:

First What is it you've spoken about before? You didnt say anything to me. Was it one of them? Maybe it was one of them! Was it? Eh? Who was it you were talking to?

Man (*generally*) There again but, you feel as if the type of event that happens during the night couldnt possibly happen at any other time. It's a bit like being a wean, when you're feart of the dark. Then come morning it's totally gone from the proceedings. So much so you can hardly remember even being feart in the first place, never mind what the fuck you were actually feart about!

Woman It's well past dawn now . . .

Pause. **Man** *nods, then sighs.*

Second Of course it is. (*Matter-of-factly.*)

First (*to* **Man**) What was it you were saying about this place?

Man *doesnt respond.*

First Eh? (*Pause.*) It's just ordinary. (*Glances around.*)

Third (*walking forwards*) Yeh.

First Is there a special history or what, attached to it, is there? (*When* **Man** *doesnt respond he crosses to* **Woman,** *indicating* **Man.**) What is he saying? Is there a special history attached somewhere? Eh? (*Returns to address* **Man.**) Is it a special history?

Third They're no going to answer you. They're using you. They're trying to get you disturbed.

First In what way? How do you mean?

Third (*shrugs*) It's for the time being. Just to make you feel as if

things have changed, as if they've altered, just to give you that
sensation. It's obvious.

First A ploy?

Third Yeh. (*Hands in pockets, he saunters, whistling tunelessly.*)

Second (*eventually*) An absolute void. Nought. There isnt any
history. Nothing has happened in the past. Nothing. They admit of
nothing at all. They say that there isnt any, that it doesnt exist; they
say that it simply doesnt exist. (**First** *is puzzled.*) They say that
history does not exist.

First In what sense?

Second (*shrugs*) You tell me!

Third *smiles, shaking his head at couple.*

Second It's just one further contradiction. It's not even a paradox.
But they wont talk about it. Not to us. And you must be cognisant of
this at all times. It's essential. It's why you can never even hope to
understand.

Third If you want to!

Second (*shrugs*) It's to be apprehending things. When you arent even
achieving that . . .

Third Indeed. (*Emphasising the point.*) I sometimes wonder what
people think about. If they think about anything. And what it is,
what the actual thing is, that they think about.

First *nods.* **Second** *smiles vaguely. Couple now stand rigidly, staring
straight ahead.* **Second** *strolls to table, peers out window as she sits
down.*

Third (*glances at wristwatch: conversationally*) I want away.

Second *doesnt respond, takes out notebook and studies a page.*

First So do I, so do I. It's really . . . It's really . . . terrible. I felt it as
well right from the start, from when I was first here. I felt it, almost
as if I could've been blooming shivering or something. That was what
I felt. I felt it, that it wouldnt be good, it wouldnt turn out to be
good. (*Glances from* **Woman** *to* **Man**, *then to* **Third**.) You know that
feeling? Eh?

Third I know what you're saying.

First It's some sort of interchange, that makes things not conducive.
(*Indicates couple, then* **Woman** *especially*.) I dont like them for
instance I just dont like them, I detest them – they make me feel as if,

as if, it's as if I'm wanting to do things, things are going to end up getting done. And I dont like it, I dont, the things that're happening, you feel like as if . . . (*Frowns. Shakes his head, fingers flexing, bunching into fists, gazing from* **Woman** *to* **Man**, *and back again.*)

Second *is now watching him. Couple still standing rigidly, apparently unaware of anything.*

First (*now sweeps his hand in direction of couple*) These blankets as well I mean they've got them and they're scabby, they're scabby, honest, they're no even clean I mean they're actually smelly they're smelly, they actually stink. (*Wrinkles his nose.*) D'you no get the whiff? It's like a bloody stench! (*Pause.*) A stench. And then too, no having any sheets I mean, imagine, no having any sheets! Just these blankets and that lumpy mattress – probably full of fleas or lice or something and them naked there underneath, the blankets. Heaven sake I mean where's their clothes? How come they've no got any clothes? How come they're naked like that?

Second *nods and* **First** *grins briefly, but still nervously.*

First You can imagine all the germs, the termites, these wee things you get in the dust, them that come flying out of old ancient bedding and stuff if you shake it – you know that way when the sun comes in the window and you can see the atmosphere, full of them, clouds of them, like a plague or something, a pestilence, a total pollution of the bloody air, and breeding everywhere you look. (*Shudders.*)

Man (*relaxes now, he calls quietly to* **Woman**) It's alright.

No one seems to hear.

First (*to* **Second**, *nervously*) But it does get to you though, eh? No think so? (*Attempts a grin.*)

Second *shows no emotion.* **Third** *stares at* **First**.

Man (*to* **Woman**, *calmly*) They're not going to harm us.

Woman (*pause, then steadily*) Yes they are.

Man *stares at her. The* **Three Inters** *dont respond.*

Second (*pause. To* **First**) Dont be misled. You mustnt be misled.

First (*controlled*) I know that.

Third It's sexual.

Second *nods.* **Man** *drops his gaze to the floor now, head bowed.*

First You just dont understand them though. Nothing at all. (*Jerks *thumb at couple*.) The way they carry on; it's as if there's a big secret they're not going to let you in on.

Second There isnt anything to understand. And there certainly isnt any secret. It's all clear and out in the open. (*Smiles to* **Third**.) He still thinks there's something missing.

Third Oh.

Second (*to* **First**) You do. You still think there's something gone astray. A key maybe. (*Smiles*.) It's funny how people think that.

Third (*glances at wristwatch, then flexes his fingers*) I'm starving. (*Smiles at* **First**:) How about you?

First (*relaxes*) Aye . . . come to think of it.

Third It's this blooming nightshift, you never seem to get a proper meal. (*Chuckles*.) I'm absolutely sick of cheese sandwiches.

First (*grins*) Yeh.

Second (*glances up from notebook*) Could you shift the mattress against the wall.

Colleagues do so at once, but casually. **Woman** *bows her head, staring at floor by her feet.* **Man** *stares out over the heads of audience.*

Second (*peers out window, sees something*) Yes. That's us. (*Matter-of-factly*.)

Man *starts and glances roundabout, clutches blanket.* **Woman** *looks to him, her hand appears from blanket as though to touch him.*

First (*to* **Third**) Okay . . . ?

Third Yeh. (*Nods to couple*.) Come on.

Man (*clutching blanket*) No! (*Stares ahead:* **Woman** *still stands staring at the floor*.)

First (*only a slight impatience*) Come on.

Man (*stubbornly*) No. (*Stands rigidly*.)

Third The two of yous, we havent got all day . . .

Woman *raises her head.* **Second** *puts away her notebook, another glance out the window as she rises, tucking the notebook into an inside pocket in her coat.* **Third** *smiles to her.* **Second** *nods, lifts flask from the table and stares at couple. Now colleagues also stare at couple.*

Freeze these positions for several seconds. Then music stops. A further pause and lights out.

End

HARDIE AND BAIRD: THE LAST DAYS

In 1978 I wrote a play for BBC Radio Scotland entitled **Hardie and Baird: The Last Days**, commissioned and directed by Stewart Conn. The actors involved were David Hayman, Tom Watson, Charles Baptiste; Iain Agnew, John Shedden, Sandy Myles; Mary Riggans, Robert Trotter, Norah Cooper and David Steuart. Unfortunately I never managed to hear the finished production properly. Although the BBC kept a copy of the manuscript it did not retain the master recording of the play, and seems to have no policy of offering the taped 'remainder' to its authors. I had taped it myself but some sort of disaster occurred a third of the way through. What I have sounds fine.

But that episode of suppressed radical history in Scotland, then its wider context, has continued to interest me. I wanted the chance to dramatise a play for theatre based on the same incident but with a shift in emphasis. I had worked with Ian Brown before and respected his wish to know a text rather than interpret it; when he offered me a commission at The Traverse I had no hesitation. **Hardie and Baird: The Last Days** was produced there in the summer of 1990:

Andrew Hardie	Simon Donald
John Baird	Tam Dean Burn
Tam Simpson	Jim Twaddale
Dr Wright/Lord President	Alexander West
Mr Small	Stuart McQuarrie
Mr Heugh	Kenneth Bryans
Bella Condy/Granny Duncan	Carol Ann Crawford

Director Ian Brown
Designer Kenny McLennan
Lighting Designer Jeanine Davies
Composer Richard Heacock

Cast

Andrew Hardie   Awaiting execution for High Treason. Just turned twenty-seven years of age, a weaver from Townhead, leader of the band of Glasgow men because of his army experience in the recent war with France.

John Baird   Awaiting execution for High Treason. Thirty/ thirty-one years of age, a weaver from Condorret. He was in overall command, with Hardie at his right hand. He had been seven years in the army.

Tam Simpson   Approximately forty-five years of age; gaoler.

Mr Heugh   Mid to late thirties; a minister.

Mr Small   Early to mid thirties; a minister.

Dr Wright   Mid fifties; a minister; walks with a limp.

Bella Condy   Nineteen years of age.

Granny Duncan   About seventy years of age.

Lord President

1st Soldier

2nd Soldier

Usher

Two Authorities

2nd Gaoler

NB The language and gesture of each speaker, as transcribed on the page, should be used as a guide, the actors should not feel hidebound by any of it.

Prologue

Can be addressed to the audience by the actor playing the parts of
Bella and Granny Duncan (but not in costume):

> Though near this place no marble statue stand,
> Nor weeping angel pointing to the spot,
> Their fame is known all through their native land,
> And never, never, shall they be forgot.

This is the last verse of a poem entitled The Dirge to Baird and
Hardie which was written by a friend of one of the two men, Daniel
Taylor of Kilsyth, to mark the occasion of their execution.
Unfortunately what he says in the verse has proved only partially
true; neither the two men nor the Scottish Insurrection in general are
ever referred to officially, while within our educational system this
part of history, like so many others connected with the Radical
movement, remains almost entirely neglected.

In the year 1820 there were eighty-eight counts of High Treason in
Scotland. There were many transportations and three weavers were
executed: James 'Purly' Wilson at Glasgow; John Baird and Andrew
Hardie at Stirling. The trials themselves were held under English
Law, in direct contravention of the 1707 Treaty of Union. This play
is based on the last days of Baird and Hardie. They were tried as
leaders of a small band of Radicals who were led into conflict with a
company of Government troops; it became known as the Battle of
Bonnymuir. The play spans the period spent by the two men, for the
most part in solitary confinement, in the dungeons of Edinburgh then
Stirling Castles.

(Pause: change of mood, but without irony:) God save the King!

Exit.

Act One Scene One

Edinburgh Castle Prison

Sudden light on **Baird** *who stands by the end of his bunk. He speaks at once in an urgent whisper which eventually settles into a more regular address:*

Baird I hope you will bear with my situation as well as possible for you can neither add to nor take away from it. I hope you will look to your own state and leave me to mine and God who is both able and willing to save to the very uttermost all that put their trust in him, he is my rock and my strong tower and my sure defence, to redeem me from sin; I will not fear what flesh can do to me. I hope you will be steadfast in the faith, studying to have your conscience void of offence towards God and towards man. Being justified by faith we are at peace with God. When He is with us, who can be against us? Go and prosper . . .

(The frown gives way, it becomes a smile:)
   Rab, go and prosper, and give my kind love to all inquiring friends. No more at present, but remain your affectionate brother, John Baird . . .

(He touches his forehead absently and frowns at the chains when they rattle, as if bewildered by them. And the lights come up on Hardie's cell.

Hardie *is seated at the tea-chest, engrossed in writing a letter.*

Baird *(continues speaking, but now more matter-of-factly)* I have nothing new to inform you of. We are well provided for. The Captain of the gaol is a very fine man; he gives us every indulgence that is in his power; he has got a very humane lady who gets our linen washed and charges nothing. The Colonel of the 80th Regiment too is one of the best; he has given us each a fine shirt as a present.

(Stops; proceeds in slightly ironic tones:)
   I am taking very well with my confinement. I am. Truly . . . I pass my time more cheerfully than you would imagine . . .

(Sudden seriousness.) But I am come to this of it now, when courage must face danger; conscience support pain; patience possess itself in the midst of discouragements.
   No more at present but remain yours until death, John Baird. *(Sits on bunk, and after a moment he speaks slowly.)* John Baird ken that's me, your brother . . . Johnnie . . . *(Stares at the floor.)*

Hardie (*continues penning letter in silence for several moments, then reads aloud, quite formally*)

Dear Mother, Sisters and Brothers, I at last received your kind and welcome letters and was truly happy to hear that you are all well, as this leaves me, thank God for his kindness to us. I am truly sorry that you did not receive my letter dated April 9th for the gentleman who examines our letters said it would be sent away. And I thanked him for his kindness, and said, 'I hope there's nothing offensive in it'; and he said, 'By no means'. So I think it will be mislaid in the post office. I asked for a little money which I knew you could ill spare. But you need not send any now for the allowance I have is quite sufficient.

I have plenty of time to reflect on my past conduct which I hope will be forgiven me through the merits of our blessed Saviour, who suffered death that our sins might be forgiven us. Give my kind compliments to my shopmates; I know they will miss me – I hope they take care of my poor bird, which you may allow them to keep if you please. I hope you have got a journeyman to my web . . . (*Pause. He reads on in silence.*)

Baird *sits up on bunk then stretches out onto his side, facing into wall, draws knees up into foetal position.*

Hardie (*resumes reading aloud*) I know you will be concerned about my unfortunate situation, but I hope God will strengthen your hearts to bear with patience whatever is his Holy Will; as for me, I am bearing it with great fortitude. He sent his only begotten son into this world who took upon himself our infirmities and suffered death for our salvation; upon this belief I build my faith and by this faith I hope to be saved.

(*He rises, walks a few steps: he returns, lifts the letter and gazes at it, reads aloud:*)

I could furnish you with many more proofs of my belief, which I shall reserve for some other time. Give my compliments to my grandfather. Give also my compliments to Margaret McKeigh; let her know I expect a letter from her shortly. (*He lays the letter down, his shoulders droop and he rubs his eyes.*)

Baird *turns onto his back, lies staring at ceiling, his breathing regular but a bit louder than* **Hardie**'s*, and he coughs, laughs quietly then starts to whistle in a breathless manner; the tune is 'Kempy's Hat'. He continues for about a minute then shuts his eyes, remains motionless.*

Hardie (*walks to end of cell, looks upwards then his head droops and his eyes close. After a few moments he flexes his shoulders, groaning: his muscles ache. He gazes upwards again, and returns to sit at the tea-chest, takes another letter, studies what he has written, scribbles something down, continues aloud, matter-of-factly:*)

My cousin was perfectly right in his conjecture with regard to my wishing that I had been killed, I really *did* wish so. When I took it into proper consideration what a rash and foolish, and unlawful action I had been guilty of, I wished I had been shot; but I sincerely repent of that rash wish and hope it will be forgiven me, and I thank God that he did not hurry me into his presence in such an unprepared state.

I informed you in the first letter how we were situated. How we were situated . . . How we had been deluded away. (*He stares at the page, then continues:*) We are now in the Castle and used with the utmost civility . . . (*He stops and stares at the page once again.*)

Sound: a couple of moments on and there comes a distant cry from somewhere far off in the prison but neither man reacts to it.

Baird (*his hands go to beneath his head; he is wide awake and deep in thought. He chuckles, it becomes a light laugh. Then he frowns. There is a pause and he smiles again*) Feyther, ye just shouldni have hit me like that . . . Ye shouldni've – it's no a way to behave, a feyther and his boy . . . (*He smiles. Then he frowns and is silent, and he stares at the ceiling.*) It's no . . . (*He frowns.*)

Hardie *walks to the end of his cell, returns to the door and waits there, his shoulder resting against it.*

Baird O God o God. (*He covers his face with both hands. He groans – angry groans. He sits suddenly up and birls roundabout, his feet clattering to the floor. He stares at his feet, he studies his chains, his breathing is heavy. He is managing to becalm himself. He closes his eyes.*)

Hardie *begins flexing his back muscles and shoulders, the top of his neck: he does a head exercise. His gaze takes in the Bible lying on the tea-chest. He continues with the exercising for a short period, then walks to lift the Bible which he thumbs through and starts to read while standing.*

Baird (*starts to smile. He coughs drily, resting his chin on the palm of his hand. He shakes his head but is not able to stop himself smiling, it becomes a quiet laugh; then his whistling once more, the breathless 'Kempy's Hat'. He stops it, he sings the opening lines of the 'Rising of the Moon':*)

> O then tell me Sean O'Farrell tell me why you hurry so
> Hush a bhuachaill hush and listen, and his cheeks were all aglow
> I bear orders from the Captain, get you ready quick and soon
> For the pikes must be together, at the rising of the moon

(*He breaks off and stares at the floor: and will eventually rest on his bunk.*)

Hardie (*turns another page of the Bible, reads a sentence and stops, then skips almost to the very end and turns pages back the way. Instead of reading he stands gazing into space. He closes the Bible, lays it on the tea-chest. He yawns and stretches quite noisily, before lifting letter which he studies prior to reading aloud*)

You will give my greatest acknowledgments to my comrade Walter, for his trouble and kindness. Any petition may be entrusted to him. (*He stops suddenly and slaps himself on the forehead and scribbles out that last sentence and once he has done so he slaps himself again and paces to the end of his cell. He stands with his back to there, shoulders drooping.*

   (*After a few moments he glances up to where a high window or grating might be. Then his gaze falls to his chains: he mutters to himself, unintelligibly at first, then he speaks aloud as if in mid-thought:*) Maggie gets my letters. (*Pause.*) She gets my compliments . . . she aye gets my compliments. (*Pause.*) There's no anything noo. Nothing. There's nothing.

(*He returns slowly onto his bunk where he stretches out, then moves onto his side, facing into the wall and mutters:*) Nothing, nothing . . . (*His breathing becomes racked, like a dry sobbing, then more regulated. He moves onto his back, stretches his arms out but they are cramped by the chains. He rubs at his wrists, gazing at the ceiling.*)

Baird *rises slowly. He walks to the end of his cell and back again, to lean his shoulders against the door. He is listening but not hearing anything. He stops listening but continues to stand there, head bowed.*

Hardie *sighs and sits up, then stands. He goes to begin writing.*

Baird *now hears something from outside and quickly lies down on his bunk.*

Two Authorities *have appeared and very very quietly they peer firstly through the keekhole in* **Baird**'s *cell, then that of* **Hardie.**

Hardie (*seems not to sense their presence, resumes*) David saith, 'If thou shouldest mark iniquity, O Lord, who shall stand? But there is forgiveness with thee, that thou mayest be feared . . .' (*He stares at what he has written then lifts Bible and checks that the last quotation is accurate before continuing.*)

Two Authorities *exit as silently as they entered.*

Hardie (*closes Bible and lifts page of letter, reads in silence, then aloud*) My cousin makes his excuse for holding so dark a prospect to me but I would be truly sorry if any of you were of another opinion, as it exactly agrees with mine. Exactly, it agrees exactly . . . with mine. (*He stares at the letter.*)

Baird *gets up and walks forwards, circles and returns to stand at door, then does the same manoeuvre once again.*

Hardie (*is scratching something out; he writes briefly and stops, chews thumbnail, resumes aloud*) Brothers and sisters, I hope you will be kind to our afflicted mother as I know my melancholy affair will sink deep in her tender heart, which already has been almost broke by the loss of our dear father and sisters and brothers who were hurried from this world; and now, by all appearances, your brother is going to be hurried away likewise, in the bloom of his youth. Therefore I hope you will lead a sober, honest and industrious life, serving God with all your heart and all your strength, and love your neighbour as you love yourself . . . (*Breaks off and sighs – but the sigh only signifies that he has been writing for some time – he flexes his back muscles and shoulders, flexes his fingers, rubs at his wrists; he continues writing in silence.*)

Baird *walks downstage, to the end of his cell, during the last bit from* **Hardie**. *When he arrives he gazes upwards as if at a high window. Then he goes to his bunk and kneels, drags out his pail from beneath and proceeds to urinate into it.*

Hardie (*studies the page then adds*) I hope some of you will not be long in writing to me. I have nothing more to add but remain your unfortunate son and brother, Andrew Hardie . . .

> In these sad moments of severe distress
> When sorrows threaten, and when dangers press
> For my defence, behold what arms are given –
> Firmness of soul, and confidence in Heaven.

PS I hope the gentleman who examines this may give notice if all letters are now being given me. (*Pause; reads in silence a moment or so.*) I would also be very happy if any of you would come to Edinburgh and see me as this liberty should now be granted. But if this is not so then I hope the gentleman may give you notice thereto, by writing in this letter . . .

(*He squints at the last bit. He considers adding something more. He folds his arms, rests his head on the palm of his hand, and he rubs at his jaw a little as if he has a slight toothache. He is very tired. He stares out and around audience; his line of vision should pass across* **Baird** *at some point. He rubs his eyes and yawns.*)

Baird (*replaces pail beneath bunk and walks to the door, leans against it. He grins, laughs briefly: he starts to take a gigantic step in the direction of the end of the cell, and takes more gigantic steps until arrival, chuckling away at himself. He about-turns, back to the door in the same style, returning in same mannered fashion, still chuckling but now going somewhat slower, and he counts in French:*) Un . . . deux . . . trois . . . quatre . . . (*This time as he passes the bunk he collapses onto it, laughing.*

(*Once his breathing has become more regular he lies on his bunk, hands beneath his head. He remains motionless. After a while he begins to sing quietly:*)

> They say ava and they gang awa
> And they leave their lassies greeting O
> O if I

(*But he stops there, lapsing into silence. He shows no emotion whatsoever.*)

This silence is held for some ten seconds: then lights dim and out.

Scene Two

Stirling Castle Dungeons

Sound of water dripping, continuous but not overpowering, and only audible from within **Baird**'s *cell. Then the solid thud of a door being shut fast.*

Hardie, Baird, Tam Simpson *and the* **Two Soldiers** *are approaching, the* **Prisoners** *in chains as before but with a change of upper clothing.* **Tam** *has his bunch of keys and the* **Soldiers** *carry muskets with bayonets fixed, but not as though envisaging an attempted escape.*

Tam Simpson (*continues alone to unlock door to the cell which is to be* **Baird**'s. *He unlocks door*) Mister Baird!

Baird *steps forwards. He exchanges nods with* **Hardie**. *He is ushered inside by* **Tam**.

Hardie (*calls just as the door is being shut*) Aw the best to ye Johnnie.

Baird Aye. And you. (*He stands with his back to the door when* **Tam** *has closed it. He stares at the interior then shuts his eyes.*)

Tam (*addresses* **Hardie** *as they continue*) That's some time to be coming back frae a trial.

Hardie *does not respond. The* **Two Soldiers** *seem disinterested.* **Tam** *unlocks cell door, ushers* **Hardie** *inside and locks it after him.*

Hardie *stands a moment then turns and faces door.*

Baird *meanwhile sits down on his bunk, very tired.*

Tam (*to* **Soldiers**, *as the trio make to leave*) Radicals by God, two o'clock in the bloody morning!

1st Soldier Yeh . . . (*Both he and* **2nd Soldier** *begin unfixing their bayonets.*)

Tam Eh? (*A glance at* **2nd Soldier**.)

2nd Soldier Mm, yeh . . . been a long day.

Tam You're no expecting that but, two o'clock in the morning, to get back frae a bloody trial.

1st Soldier Did ye say something about a drink my friend . . . ?

Tam (*grins and winks at* **2nd Soldier**) Thirsty eh!

2nd Soldier *smiles but then gives an amused glance to his comrade when* **Tam** *is not looking.*

Hardie *and* **Baird** *surveying their cells now.* **Baird** *is less interested than* **Hardie** *who walks the length of his, gazing this way and that; he rubs at his jaw then rubs at his eyes, covers his face with both hands.*

Baird (*leans over to peer beneath the bunk and sees his pail; he pulls it out and looks inside, seeing it to be empty, then he pushes it back and becomes aware of the water dripping*) Aw God. (*He stares in the direction of it, groans.*)

Hardie *begins breathing loudly and regularly. He flexes his shoulders. He turns to his bunk, kneels to see his pail beneath it which he drags out to look inside. Then he sits down on the bunk.*

Baird (*tired frustration*) Fucking dripping water . . . Whh! Tch. (*Rubs at the back of his neck and flexes his shoulders. He raises himself to stretch along on the bunk and he sighs.*) Aw dear . . . (*He closes his eyes and within seconds begins sleeping.*)

Hardie *lies down and pulls the blanket up to his chin, moves onto his side.*

Lights out.

Scene Three

Tam *unlocks the door of* **Hardie***'s cell. He is returning* **Hardie***'s slops pail.*

Lights: but only dimly on **Baird***'s cell.* **Baird** *is sleeping on his side, facing into the wall; an empty porridge bowl is on the floor nearby the bunk.* **Hardie** *is lying on his bunk, reading a book: his Bible is on the floor next to the bowl of porridge which sits on the floor.*

Tam (*enters cell, puts the pail down*) Reading already by God, eh!

Hardie (*without lifting his head*) The porridge was freezing cauld. And it was lumpy as well.

Tam What . . . (*Lifting the bowl and peering into it.*)

Hardie I'm no wanting it.

Tam. Come on. You've got to eat.

Hardie (*pause*) Gie it to somebody needing it up the sterr.

Tam (*irritated*) There's naebody needing it up the sterr! (*Glares at him.*) You dae too much grumping. Ye dae. (*Pause.*) Look it's no my fault: it goes cauld by the time I get doon here. The kitchen's miles away. (**Hardie** *is not responding.*) It's no my fault. (*Pause.*) You didni eat yesterday either.

Hardie (*after a moment*) I'm no hungry.

Tam Ach!

Hardie Is there any letters for me? (*Still not taking his gaze from the book.*)

Bring the lights in **Baird***'s cell up to the equivalent of those in* **Hardie***'s.* **Baird** *has moved onto his back, he has his eyes open, his hands beneath his head.*

Tam Naw. And neither there will be noo, no till eftir yous all get sentenced.

Hardie What about something to write on then? Or is that still no allowed either. I thought they were supposed to be gieing ye stuff in for me?

Tam Who telt you that? There's nae point gieing ye stuff in for writing if your letters are stopped.

Hardie *grunts.*

Tam (*angrily*) Aye well you go and tell their Lordships then eh! Ye dae enough damn blethering when ye want tae! (*Pause.*) Are ye gonni eat this grub? (*Pause.*) Aye well suit yoursel it's just you that suffers. (*Turns to leave, then glances back at* **Hardie**.) They canni say it's my fault. God sake!

Hardie (*firmly but without raising his voice: he gazes at* **Tam**) I'd prefer ye no tae blaspheme Tam.

Tam (*glowering at him*) Aye much good it does ye! (*Makes to exit with the bowl.*)

Hardie What about exercising, have we no even to get a walk round the castle yard?

Tam How dae I know! I just dae what I'm telt!

Hardie *turns from him, resumes reading.*

Tam *shakes his head in great irritation: opens cell door and steps out, locks and bolts it.* **Hardie** *continues reading.*

Baird (*hears sound of* **Tam**'s *keys and gets quickly onto his feet to listen at door, stays listening for several seconds until sure no one is coming to his cell. He stops listening and leans against the door. Then he whispers loudly through clenched teeth*) Will ye stoap up the fucking wattir! Eh! Will ye! (*He covers his eyes with his hands and groans.*) Ohhhh Jesus, ohh Jesus, Jesus Christ.

Hardie *has read something he likes very much. He grins and shakes his head. He becomes serious, he studies the page, frowns then shuts his eyes as though to memorise a line or two.*

Baird (*sits down on the floor with his back resting against the cell door. He speaks matter-of-factly*) Ken I'm no gonni take this ye know. I'm no. I'm no gonni take it. I'm just no. I'm no. (*He sits staring at his feet: he leans to scratch his ankle.*)

Hardie *closes the Bible, rises, walks the length of the cell and back, then forwards again and stands downstage.*

Baird (*speaks as though reciting a poem*) When I was a young boy my heart was so full. (*Five second pause.*) When I was a young boy . . .

(*He massages his feet, hums a tune for a few moments – the tune is not intelligible.*)

Hardie *kneels; folds his arms, head bowed, eyes closed as if praying.*

Baird (*begins singing midway through the song 'There's bound to be a row'*)

> . . . there's bound to be a row.
> There's bound to be a row, there's bound to be a row
> I do all my life to please my wife but there's bound to be a
> row
> She takes in a ludger, he's single bye the bye
> And I've to make room for him and on the sofa lie

(*He lapses into silence, staring at his feet.*)

Hardie *now stretches out on the floor to begin doing a series of press-ups, about seven or eight. Then he lies on his front, recovering his breath.*

Lights dim.

Baird (*eventually gazes upwards in the direction of the water dripping. He speaks slowly*) They had the iron oan me ken stones of iron, laid on me, on ma chest . . . Imagine that, eh Rab! Hh . . . (*Shake of the head.*) Stones of iron oan ma chest . . . (*And he whispers.*) Fuck . . . ! (*Eventually he starts flexing his neck and shoulders.*)

Hardie *raises himself and does another three or four press-ups, then goes to his bunk and lies down, hands behind his head, gazing at the ceiling.*

Baird *gets to his feet, sits heavily down on his bunk, then hears a sound from outside the cell.* **Tam** *is on his way though not yet in view.*

Tam *enters carrying a tray, bread and water for two. He peers in the keekhole of* **Baird**'s *cell door.* **Baird** *has heard him come and is waiting.* **Tam** *unbolts and unlocks door, enters with the tray.*

Tam Good day to ye John.

Baird Aye Tam.

Tam Hungry?

Baird No bad . . . (*Drinks water.*) Good water. (*He lifts the bread and looks at it, sniffs.*) Stale. (*Bites a small bit and chews.*) Nae sign of the auld wummin coming back yet? Or young Bella?

Tam It'd be the same breid if they were here or no.

Baird Would it?

Tam Aye. Anywey, Bella Condy's got nothing to dae with the kitchen. (*Takes a book from his pocket and gives him it.*) A book . . .

Baird *frowns at title as though slight difficulty in reading it.*

Tam One of the clergy left it for ye.

Baird (*nods, opens book and reads aloud, without any irony whatsoever*) Some thoughts on the worth of man . . . (*He glances at* **Tam** *who watches non-committally as* **Baird** *reads for a moment. Then* **Baird** *lays the book down.*) Nae news Tam?

Tam Whit kinda news?

Baird *just looks at him.*

Tam I've no been doon the toon for a couple a nights.

Baird *still just looks at him.*

Tam I dont get to hear everything ye know.

Baird (*pause. Then he nods*) How's the lads up the sterr?

Tam Fine, far as I hear.

Baird Are they getting letters?

Tam Aw I wouldni think so, no if yous urni. (*Pause.*) Truly, I dont. (*Indicates book.*) If ye dont want the book I'll take it away.

Baird Och naw leave it wi me, ken for the time being.

Tam *walks the length of the cell, peering this way and that.*

Baird (*watches him*) Ye looking for something?

Tam Naw.

Baird *nods, leafs through pages of the book, but then he shuts it again. And he sighs.*

Tam (*gazes at him for a moment before speaking*) Nae use in worrying about the Sentencing. You'll find oot soon enough.

Baird (*immediate irritation*) What? Find oot what! (*Shakes his head.*) God's truth Tam, I've known *that* since the sixth of fucking April.

Tam *stares at him.*

Baird Come on.

Tam But ye canni know it for sure.

Baird *just looking at him.*

Tam You've got to be able to hope for something.

Baird Tam Tam . . . what's for breakfast . . .

Tam (*angrily*) Ach! (*Strides to door, collects tray as he goes. Then he halts and turns to* **Baird**.) You'll be getting some visitors later.

Baird Visitors . . .

Tam Some of the clergy're coming in . . . Nae doubt they'll be visiting down here.

Baird *does not respond.*

Tam Aye well you're aye moaning about folk getting to see ye!

Baird (*irritation obvious, but never raises his voice*) Aye real visitors! Friends. That's who I was talking aboot – friends, or relations.

Tam The clergy's good people.

Baird I'm no wanting to get into any argy bargy wi you Tam. I dont, I just want a bit of peace, alright? A bit of fucking peace. So just away and get on with your work; ken your masters dont pey ye for blethering wi politicals.

Tam *exits and slams shut the door.*

Baird *gets onto his feet: the interchange has upset him a bit. He paces downstage and eventually sits on the floor. He turns and lifts the book from the bunk and glances at the initial pages, then chips it back onto the bunk. He leans against the cell door.*

Lights dim, then out.

Sound of a clock chiming somewhere, the water still dripping.

Scene Four

Lights.

Hardie *is kneeling, urinating into his bucket. He returns pail beneath the bunk and lifts a book, but closes it and moves to begin a series of press-ups, or similar exercising.*

Baird (*resting on the bunk, eyes open, deep in thought. Occasionally he chuckles. He closes his eyes but is still registering amusement. Then he sings the following lines from 'There's bound to be a row'*)

She takes in a ludger, he's single bye the bye
And I've to make room for him and on the sofa lie
It's the meat to he and to me the bones and it doesni seem
right somehow

(*He becomes silent, stares ahead. He smiles suddenly, shakes his head: he sighs.*) I'm no wanting things, I'm no needing them ken they're nothing to me, they're no anything, them, they're no anything. I'm in nae need. (*Shrugs.*)

Hardie *has now stopped exercising and lies on the floor recuperating.*

Baird (*rises and walks downstage and returns, then back and forwards for a spell and he chants the lines*)

She takes in a ludger, he's single bye the bye
And I've to make room for him and on the sofa lie

(*He continues pacing in silence. Then when he arrives by the door he halts and listens intently. The* **Ministers** *can be heard from afar, chatting together.* **Baird** *quickly gets onto his bunk, pulls blanket up to his chin and turns onto his side, feigning sleep.*

Dr Wright, Mr Small *and* **Mr Heugh** *appear, accompanied by* **Tam.** *They walk to the door of* **Baird**'s *cell and there they listen at the keekhole.* **Tam** *unlocks the door quietly and he and* **Dr Wright** *peer inside, seeing* **Baird** *to be 'asleep'. They return outside.*

Dr Wright Sleeping.

The **Three Ministers** *glance at one another.*

Mr Heugh Let's leave him be.

Mr Small If ye think so Mister Heugh.

Mr Heugh I do. God knows any rest must be welcome.

Dr Wright Aye.

Tam *locks up.*

Baird *lifts his head to listen for a few moments. He collects his book from the floor at the side of the bunk and will read for a spell: during the scene in* **Hardie**'s *cell with the* **Ministers** *he will rise and stroll about. Eventually he settles to read while resting on his bunk.*

Tam *indicates the keekhole of* **Hardie**'s *cell door to the trio.* **Mr Small** *is the one to look inside.*

Mr Small (*whispers*) He's lying flat on the floor . . .

Hardie *has been lying on the floor after exercising but when he hears the key in the lock he gets quickly to his feet, stands with his hands behind his back in a formal attitude.*

Dr Wright *nods in reply to* **Mr Small**. **Mr Heugh** *does not respond. Then* **Tam** *ushers the ministers inside, closing the door behind them. He exits.*

Dr Wright We're no disturbing ye eh lad, ken we're a wee bit late the night.

Hardie Naw, it's fine.

Mr Small (*glances to* **Dr Wright** *before speaking*) You were lying flat on the floor.

Hardie Aye, I'd just been doing my exercises Mister Small. I was about to start reading.

Mr Small I see. (*But not really convinced.*)

Hardie It helps me get to sleep.

Mr Small Ah. (*Almost an accusation.*) So you're no sleeping then?

Hardie No always, naw.

Mr Small Your mind's troubled? You're dwelling on your misfortunes?

Hardie (*pause*) I thank God for my misfortunes. I dae. (*Glances at the other two ministers.*) Truly, I dae. (*Smiles.*) Blest the dungeon – blest the dungeon which thus led to heaven.

Dr Wright You mean that lad?

Hardie I'm feeling a lot easier since last I saw ye.

Mr Heugh (*gravely*) You're prepared for the sentencing then Andy?

Hardie Aye . . . (*Gestures at his bunk.*) Eh Doctor Wright . . . if you'll take a sit down.

Dr Wright I will lad, thank you. (*Sits.*) Tam Simpson was saying you're no always eating.

Hardie (*shrugs*) I'm just no always that hungry.

Dr Wright (*studies him a moment*) Aye well it's no a thing to be doing without, your food. (*His attention distracted by the book lying nearby: he picks it up and begins reading, absently.*)

Mr Heugh You'll hae a deal to contend with. You'll need to keep up your strength.

Hardie God'll grant me the strength.

Mr Small Amen tae that.

Mr Heugh (*after a pause*) How are ye for ink and writing materials?

Hardie (*shrugs*) Letters have been cancelled till further notice . . .

Mr Heugh Again! (*Glances at his companions.*)

Mr Small (*ironic*) It would seem to be the case Mister Heugh, aye. (*Then a glance at* **Hardie**.) So the sentencing isni preying on your mind then?

Hardie I just wish it was ower and done wi.

Mr Small Mm.

Mr Heugh Is there anything else ye're in need of?

Hardie (*pause*) There's the candles right enough I mean if they burn out . . . I sometimes wonder about that. Cause I'm no sleeping at the usual hours and if I wisni able to get reading . . .

Mr Heugh Dont worry about it. The gaoler keeps his eye on that. We'll remind him though if it makes ye easier.

Dr Wright (*absently*) The light shineth in darkness.

Hardie Aye Doctor Wright. (*Then quickly but respectfully.*) Be nae candles without God but, surely . . . All things were made by him.

Dr Wright (*finishes quote while laying down the book*) And without him was not anything made that was made.

Hardie Aye.

Dr Wright (*approvingly*) You're studying the scriptures.

Hardie It's no a hardship Doctor Wright. I've aye been a reader anywey.

Mr Heugh (*to* **Dr Wright**) He used to attend the Mechanics Institute.

Dr Wright Is that right?

Hardie Aye.

Mr Heugh (*to* **Hardie**) You were saying to me about the star-gazing . . . ? (*To* **Dr Wright**.) Some of them were gonni be going out on hikes.

Hardie We were getting the loan of a telescope.

Dr Wright The loan of a telescope . . .

Hardie They can capture merr than a hunner times the amount of light your eye can. Which means ye can see a hunner times merr into the sky, deeper I mean.

Mr Small Where were ye getting the loan of a telescope?

Hardie (*shrugs*) The Institute I suppose.

Mr Small The Institute, aye, and who would be taking charge of it?

Hardie Taking charge of it . . . ?

Dr Wright (*patiently*) Ken what Mister Small's meaning there is how these telescopes are valuable instruments lad, it wouldni do to be treating them in a way that wasni serious.

Mr Small I was also beginning to wonder about your web, if you'd ever fit in the time to do your work? (*With a brief glance at* **Mr Heugh** *then he nods at* **Dr Wright**.)

Hardie *stares at the floor.*

Mr Heugh (*shakes his head. He turns suddenly to* **Hardie**) And have ye heard the news from Greenock?

Mr Small Mister Heugh . . . ! We're no here to impart information to prisoners. (*A look to* **Dr Wright**.)

Mr Heugh (*glances at* **Dr Wright**) Ach ye know how this sort of news travels Doctor Wright, it's as well coming frae us as Tam Simpson or auld Granny Duncan!

Mr Small That's no an argument.

Dr Wright It isni Mister Heugh.

Mr Heugh But the word's everywhere. (*And to* **Hardie**:) There's been an incident doon at Greenock, between the townsfolk and the military.

Hardie What kinda incident?

Mr Heugh Mind now these are early reports Andy but it seems to be fighting.

Dr Wright It's a bad business: there's nae good'll come of it.

Mr Small A riot!

Mr Heugh No quite the words I heard Mister Small. (*Then to* **Hardie**:) What they're saying in the toon is how a crowd are supposed to've stoned a company of soldiers. Stoned them. They were trying to cart a half dozen weavers aff to gaol.

Hardie What . . . ?

Mr Small (*impatiently*) A mob attacked the military, that's what's happened. They attacked the military while they were going aboot their lawful business. The way matters are in the country the now I would hardly've thought it the sort of news to be spreading like this – you would think the affair delighted ye.

Mr Heugh (*quickly*) The affair doesni delight me minister, I just think Mister Hardie should be availed of the information.

Hardie The townsfolk fighting the soldiers – to set free the weavers?

Mr Heugh That's what they're saying, aye.

Hardie *Excited laugh.*

Mr Small (*impatient sigh and a look to* **Dr Wright**) Aye Mister Heugh, a mob attacks a company of soliders – fine grounds for amusement.

Dr Wright (*gravely*) Mister Heugh.

Mr Heugh (*to* **Dr Wright**) The news is everywhere.

Hardie (*has paced slowly to the far end of his cell and he stands there for some time, deep in thought. He returns to the cell door, continues pacing for a short while. The sound of a clock chiming somewhere, but vaguely. He rubs at his face, frustration, his chains rattle: and he turns to the* **Ministers**) They'll have had nae right to arrest them in the first place. It's aye the way of it but, it's how this government treat ordinary working men. (*His fists clench.*)

Mr Small There can never be any excuse for arms Mister Hardie. True justice, true liberty, true religion; never a one required weapons of destruction.

Mr Heugh Ho!

Mr Small Aye Mister Heugh!

Dr Wright (*clears throat*) Ken one side doesni hae the haud on truth Mister Heugh, let's not forget that.

Mr Heugh I'm hardly likely to Doctor Wright.

Mr Small There are two sides to every story.

Mr Heugh (*just barely controlling his annoyance*) Thanks for reminding me. (*Turns abruptly.*) And there's never any call to open up wi muskets on a crowd of unarmed men. It fair does me sick to hear o it.

Mr Small When?

Mr Heugh When! There can never be any justification for such action. And them responsible will answer for it – before God, if no in this world.

Dr Wright *glances from one colleague to the other.*

Mr Small Ye need not tell me about God, minister.

Mr Heugh *stands staring at him.*

Mr Small Ye need not tell me about God.

Mr Heugh *now accepts by a nod of the head that he is in the wrong.*

Mr Small We shall all come before Him.

Dr Wright Amen . . .

Mr Heugh *is still emotional from the confrontation.*

Mr Small The laws of the land are the laws of the land.

Mr Heugh (*speaks in spite of himself*) Bad laws!

Mr Small Laws.

Hardie Laws only count for them that've framed them, if you've no had any say in the framing of them then they've got nothing to do with ye.

Mr Small *looks at him with the utmost contempt.* **Mr Heugh** *witnesses him doing so and shakes his head in disgust.*

Dr Wright Eh ministers . . . (*Sharply, and the other two take heed.* **Dr Wright** *rises from the bunk and walks downstage as though to stretch his legs. He stands a moment, glances at his watch, then to* **Hardie**:) Have ye heard from your mother? (*Pause.*) Eh?

Hardie (*eventually*) No for a while. Letters've aw been cancelled.

Dr Wright O aye, aye. (*Sudden interest.*) Your faimly attend Doctor Chalmers's services I'm telt.

Hardie (*quietly*) Aye.

Dr Wright Mm . . .

Hardie He's a great man.

Dr Wright Aye . . .

Mr Small *should convey he has no particular regard for either Doctor Chalmers or* **Hardie**'s *family.*

Hardie His church is packed, people come frae aw over.

Dr Wright Mm.

Mr Heugh So you'll no know how she's keeping then Andy?

Hardie My mother, naw, but she's alright as far as I've been telt. But I dont suppose I've been telt everything . . .

Mr Heugh Naw, I dont suppose . . .

Hardie She's had a hard time of it, wi my feyther being deid these last few years. My granpa's went to stay with her for a wee bit.

Dr Wright Your granpa?

Hardie Aye.

Mr Heugh He a weaver as well?

Hardie Aye. (*Sniffs; and this is an aid to defiance.*) Him and James Wilson were acquainted at ane time.

Mr Small (*sharply*) Were they really . . .

Mr Heugh *exasperation with his colleague is evident.*

Hardie (*to Mr Heugh*) He knew Thomas Muir as well Mister Heugh, back in the auld days, they used to attend meetings the gether.

Mr Small Indeed.

Hardie Universal suffrage and annual parliament, the natural rights of *all* people, they were aye the thing.

Mr Small (*hand raised immediately*) No speechifying just now Mister Hardie, if ye please. (*Pauses. His gaze also takes in **Mr Heugh** here.*) There can never be any valid cause for the raising of arms.

Mr Heugh *shows irritation at this – but not necessarily because he rejects the point, he is more irritated that it should be aired at this time.*

Dr Wright (*generally*) The wrath of man worketh not the righteousness of God.

Hardie Aye but surely that must cut both ways, surely that must cut both ways.

Mr Small (*enunciates every syllable*) There exist legitimate and adequate sources for the upkeep of law and order within society Mister Hardie: sometimes they've got to be employed by the appropriate authorities, especially when there's folk bent on the flouting of them, as you yourself have got good reason to beware.

Mr Heugh *His exasperation again. He turns away.*

Dr Wright (*pause*) Have you looked yet at James eh Andrew, in the New Testament, I'm thinking particular on the first chapters.

Mr Heugh (*while staring off*) A hearer of the word and not a doer.

Mr Small *glances at his back.*

Dr Wright Chapter four, he that speaketh evil of his brother and judgeth his brother, speaketh evil of the law, and judgeth the law: but if thou judge the law, thou art not a doer of the law, but a judge. And we are not judges, we are men, we are simple mortal beings.

Mr Heugh (*is nodding agreement: continues train of thought directly to* **Hardie**) James also talks about how the rich will weep and howl, and the way that they keep back a proper living wage from their labourers in the field.

Hardie I know.

Dr Wright (*glances at his watch once again*) We called in on John Baird earlier but he was sleeping and we thought it best no to wake him. (*Glances at the ministers.*)

Mr Small *looks at his own fob watch.*

Dr Wright (*to* **Mr Heugh**) It is late . . .

Mr Heugh *nods.*

Hardie I thank ye all for coming.

Dr Wright Not at all.

Hardie Thanks but, all the same.

Mr Small We have the obligation Mister Hardie, and we accede to it.

Mr Heugh God go with you for the sentencing Andy.

Hardie When he's with me who can be against me?

Mr Small Ye continue to admire his works?

Hardie With his own assistance Mister Small.

Dr Wright Long suffering and slow to anger . . .

Hardie He's my rock.

Mr Small And pray. Pray. Continue to pray. The son of man himself died that we might live. We pray for ye. (*He stares at* **Hardie**.)

Mr Heugh (*places his hand on* **Hardie**'*s shoulder*) Keep your courage. The Lord'll sustain ye, through the coming ordeal Andy, he'll sustain ye, he'll look out for ye . . .

Dr Wright Amen tae that.

Mr Small (*steps to door and calls*) Gaoler!

Tam *appears.*

Baird *also hears the call and* **Tam**'*s footsteps and he goes to listen at the cell door, the book in his hand.*

The **Ministers** *walk ahead of* **Tam**, *glancing at* **Baird**'*s cell door when they pass it. As they vanish from view* **Mr Small** *can be heard speaking, what he says is not intelligible.*

But **Baird** *is still by his door as if straining to hear.*

Hardie *stares up at the high window, then his head droops, his eyes shut.*

There are no sounds now, except for the breathing of the **Prisoners** *and the water dripping.*

Lights dim.

Baird *turns at once and he stares downstage. He turns again to listen by the cell door.*

Lights out.

Scene Five

Lights: dimly in **Baird**'*s cell only.* **Hardie** *will sleep throughout this scene.*

Bella Condy *is standing motionless in* **Baird**'*s cell. She is gazing at him as he lies asleep beneath his blanket. He now turns over onto his side.*

Bella (*whispers*) Johnnie. Johnnie.

Baird (*eventually opens his eyes, raises his head, sees her. His surprise is evident but very muted*) Bella? (*She is smiling.*) Bella?

Bella How are ye Johnnie?

Baird (*a bit hoarsely*) I'm fine. How are you? How was your auntie?

Bella Oh she was awright. She's aye awright – auld besom that she is.

Baird *rubs his eyes.*

Bella You're looking tired.

Baird I am tired. It's a queer thing, ye sit about doing nothing aw day. When did ye come back?

Bella (*smiles*) Yesterday morning.

Baird Did ye. (*He is suddenly aware of himself and swiftly checks that the blanket is covering his decency.*)

Bella Ye're sleeping though eh.

Baird Aye, God, I canni stop. (*Tails off.*) You're looking well yourself Bella . . . (*Nods his head formally.*) I mean Miss Condy . . .

Bella Tch!

Baird (*chuckles*) Well ye are a Miss ken are ye no!

Bella Tch.

Baird Well ye are! Unless ye got merrit while ye were away supposed tae be seeing that auld auntie of yours! Here, will ye turn your head a minute while I get out of the bunk. (**Bella** *does so and* **Baird** *swings himself out, adjusting his trousers.*) A gentleman shouldni receive a lady in his bed! (*He grins. He coughs briefly.*)

Bella Oh shut up you. And where's the gentleman anywey, I dont see ane!

Baird (*just laughs quietly. There is a gap now in the conversation which could become awkward. Eventually he speaks*) It's good to see ye Bella.

Bella *gazes up at him.*

Baird So how are ye? How's your uncle's tumshies!

Bella Oh his tumshies're fine except for these thievin sheep getting in the field and eating them – it sends him daft! He goes rushing about with a big stick belting them.

Baird (*chuckles*) Ach he shouldni go belting them, poor auld sheep, they're just dumb beasts.

Bella Oh they're no so dumb. They're no! (*She smiles but the smile soon goes. She is aware of* **Baird** *gazing at her and becomes self-conscious: she adjusts her clothing as a reflex action.*)

Baird (*turns from her. He walks a step or two, sighs, rubs his* *forehead. He gazes at her and smiles, and speaks a moment later*) I never really knew the wummin in my faimly very well. I didni. I was just away too long. (*Absently.*) So ye dont know how to act, wi wummin I mean ken it makes ye aw fingers and thumbs and, ach, knees and elbows, it makes ye aw sort of – jaggy.

Bella Jaggy!

Baird Well ye just . . . Dont laugh at me.

Bella I'm no.

Baird (*shrugs*) Ye jist dont know the wey ye've to behave ken what ye're supposed to dae, if you're in a particular eh sort of company. I mind during the war there we were down near the border of Belgium and we had to go tae (*Stops abruptly and frowns.*) You dont want to hear about this.

Bella I dae.

Baird Naw, ye dont.

Bella I dae Johnnie, I like hearing stories when ye tell them.

Baird No that yin ye dont, it's just bloody boring. (*Then absently but with irony.*) I'm just getting a bit auld, ken? Doatty . . . I'm getting doatty . . . (*He smiles briefly.* **Bella** *just gazes at him. He shakes his head and turns from her.*)

Bella Dont be so hard on yoursel, it's nae good.

Baird (*pause*) Ye been in to see any of the Condorret boys, ken wee Eck?

Bella (*shakes her head*) I'll no get the chance, I've only got the few minutes spare. (*Glances at the door.*) There was a man into Stirling yesterday wanting to visit Andy.

Baird Was there?

Bella They wouldni let him of course. Poor fella, he wasni even able to stey the night, he had his work to go to in the morning. It's Glasgow he steys.

Baird Did ye find out what his name was?

Bella Naw.

Baird Ye sure noo Bella?

Bella I'd a minded.

Baird *nods.*

Bella Coming aw that way for nothing . . . It seems like they're hauding back, the authorities . . .

Baird Aye – for George the Fournicator to get sent the divided parts o us! – so's he can stick them on the palace spikes tae amuse the court. Maybe that's treason an aw Bella eh! Better gie Sidmouth a shout.

Bella *is upset by this.*

Baird Bella . . . dont take it hard like this, dont . . .

Bella *glances away from him, her hand to her brow.*

Baird Bella . . .

She half turns to face him again. They gaze at each other.

Baird (*is first to drop his gaze. He turns and walks downstage, stares up at the high window. He turns to face her again*) It is a pity but, ken wi him coming aw that wey, Andy's visitor, no tae get let in, him having to go aw the wey hame again.

Bella I know.

Baird I hope he didni have to walk it.

Bella Poor Andy. And his lassie as well . . . she must be taking it bad.

Baird Aye.

Bella A visitor would have been good for him. (*Shakes head.*)

Baird Is he alright?

Bella I've no had the chance to see him yet and I'm no sure if I will noo or no . . . there's jist so much to dae ower in the hospital.

Baird (*pause*) He's a good man Andy.

Bella (*sharp look at him*) So are you.

Baird Aye but he's eh . . . Me and him are different, ken? We were never acquainted neither, no tae the night in question. The authorities seem to think we wur cause we baith fought against Napoleon! But we didni. I never knew any of them frae Glasgow. Nane of us did, us frae the village. (*Sudden smile.*) Ah they were a good bunch but, the lot of them; they marched and they fought like a damn regiment! That was whit the officer-in-charge of the Hussars says for his testimony at the trial. And it wis good of him. He was a real soldier him, he didni have to say it, he didni . . . (*Turns his head from her and is immediately close to tears, his hand to his eyes etc.*)

What's the weather like? Hard tae tell in this place, aye so bloody damp!

Bella Are ye alright?

Baird Aye. (*Attempted irony.*) Is the sun shining that bright wey?

Bella It's been hot.

Baird Has it! And what's been happening? Anything?

Bella *does not respond.*

Baird Eh Bella?

Bella What like?

Baird I dont know – you're supposed to tell me! (**Bella** *remains silent and he laughs briefly.*) You'd never get a job for Sidmouth or them, first thing a spy has to dae is tae listen and look at whit's going on roundabout. And if it isni going the wey ye want it ye just go bloody oot and dae it yoursel!

That wis the wey of it wi us more or less. Ken? We were aw kidded on, thousands of us! (*Grins.*) I'm no jist meaning us in here! They made goats out of us, the government. Goats! (*Grins. Shakes his head.*)

Bella (*angrily*) Dont be saying that, dont.

Baird *stares at her.* **Bella** *is very upset.*

Bella Jist dont be saying that.

Baird *passes his hand over his forehead, then he stares at her again.*

Bella Oh Johnnie.

Baird *is unable to speak.*

Bella (*a wee bit more urgency now*) Johnnie.

Baird *staring at her.*

Lights out.

Scene Six

Lights dim.

Both men are sleeping. Then **Baird** *awakens and after a moment he* *rises and walks to stand gazing upwards at the high window for a time.*

Lights out.

Scene Seven

Sound of kettle drums fade in eventually; then the vague bustling noises of a fairly crowded courtroom.

The Courtroom

Lights and silence.

Hardie *and* **Baird** *stand at opposite sides of the stage, facing at an angle away from each other. Downstage from them stand the* **Two Soldiers** *in an aggressive posture, muskets held at the ready with bayonets fixed: they stare at audience.* **Usher** *stands at attention by the entrance.*

Lord President *enters. He walks to centrestage and stands downstage from* **Hardie** *and* **Baird**, *but not as far so as the* **Two Soldiers**.

Usher (*calls*) Pray silence for the Lord President.

Lord President (*reads the names of the twenty-two prisoners from a scroll, addressing the audience*) Andrew Hardie, John Baird, Jem Cleland, Thomas MacCulloch; Benjamin Moir, Alan Murchie, Alexander Latimer; Alexander Johnstone, Andrew White, David Thomson, James Wright; William Clackson, Thomas Pink or Pike; Robert Gray, Alexander Hart, John Barr, William Smith; Thomas MacFarlane, John Anderston, William Crawford, John MacMillan, Andrew Dawson.

Sound of muttering in court: quelled when the **Usher** *walks forwards a pace and glances from side to side. He returns.*

Lord President (*continuing*) You present a melancholy spectacle. Two and twenty subjects of this country who have forfeited their lives to justice; a spectacle I believe unexampled in this country, such at least *I* never witnessed and trust in God never shall again. The crime of which you are convicted is the crime of High Treason, a crime the highest known to law, and the highest, I may say, which can be known to a reflecting mind.

At the same time I am well aware that from the delusion practised against you, and from the principles some of you have imbibed, you may view this in a different light, that you may consider yourselves not as victims of justice but as martyrs for liberty.

Repentance alone is not sufficient. Remember that you also have to appear before God who is possessed of not only infinite mercy but of inflexible justice; and that both must be satisfied by us miserable sinners.

It remains for me to pronounce against one and all of you the last awful sentence of the law.

Both the **Soldiers** *and the* **Usher** *brace themselves.*

Lord President (*stares at both prisoners*) In regard to you Andrew Hardie and John Baird, I can hold out little or no hope of mercy. You were selected for trial as the leaders of that band in which you were associated. You were convicted after a full and fair trial, and it is utterly impossible to suppose, considering the convulsions into which this country was thrown, that the Crown must not feel the necessity of making some terrible example.

The sentence of the law is that you, and each and every one of you, be taken to the place from whence you came, and that you be drawn on a hurdle to the place of execution, and there be hung by the neck until you are dead, and afterwards . . .

A sudden outbreak of muttering in the court, amid which a woman's cry can be heard distinctly.

Lord President (*acknowledges the interruption only by a sideways glance to where her cry came from. And he continues at once*) . . . and afterwards your head severed from your body, and your body divided into four quarters to be disposed of as His Majesty may direct – and may God – in His infinite goodness, have mercy on your souls.

Woman can be heard moaning briefly.

Lord President (*now relaxes a little for the concluding remarks*) I must add that it is apparent there existed in April last a dangerous conspiracy which extended over five Scottish counties, a thing unparalleled in the manufacturing districts. Under the pretence of reformation and redress of grievances the April rising was aimed at subverting the constitution and Government of the country by law established. There can surely be no question of the great and abominable crimes undoubtedly intended by the Radicals. I may add that whatever little petty grievances or whatever the trifling alterations to the constitution sought by them, the constitution remains without fear of contradiction, the best, the wisest, and the freest, that the sun ever saw. God save the King.

Usher God save the King!

The **Soldiers** *again brace themselves.*

Lord President *stands gazing at the audience for a moment, then turns and walks off, followed by* **Hardie** *and* **Baird**, *with the* **Two Soldiers** *following at the rear. Lastly comes the* **Usher**. *Now fade in the sound of the kettle drum.*

Lights: wait for a few moments with the stage empty, then out.

Sound of the kettle drum continues for a time.

Scene Eight

Lights: dimly in **Hardie**'s *cell. He lies on his bunk reading the Bible (the 51st Psalm).* **Baird** *is meanwhile asleep on his side.*

Hardie (*reads aloud in a breathless manner, occasionally closing his eyes as if attempting to memorise the lines:*)

> After thy loving kindness, Lord have mercy upon me:
> For thy compassions great, blot out all mine iniquity
> Me cleanse from sin, and thoroughly wash from mine iniquity.
> For my transgressions I confess; my sin I ever see.
> 'Gainst thee, thee only, have I sinn'd, in thy sight done this ill;
> That when thou speak'st thou may'st be just, and clear in
>   judging still.
> Behold, I in iniquity was form'd the womb within;
> My mother also me conceiv'd in guiltiness and sin
> Behold, thou in the inward parts with truth delighted art;
> And wisdom thou shalt make me know within the hidden
>   part.
> Do thou with hyssop sprinkle me . . .

(*Pause: he stares at the text, frowns.*) ' . . . with hyssop sprinkle me'. Hyssop. Hyssop . . . (*And he changes the vowel sound of the 'y' as in 'Hill' with the 'y' as in 'High' on the third usage of the term. He continues to gaze at the text for several seconds. He lays the Bible on the floor and sits for a moment, then bows his head and shuts his eyes; he speaks as in prayer:*)

For my transgressions I confess; my sin I ever see. Against thee only have I sinn'd, pray God forgive me, Andrew Hardie, Amen.

He stretches out, tugs the blanket over himself, then right over his head. He tries to sleep but cannot settle: he turns onto his other side and starts muttering unintelligibly for a short period. Then he lies on his back, motionless, still with the blanket over his head. Moments later he throws the blanket off and gets out the bunk and onto his feet. He embarks on a series of press-ups. Eventually he stops and lies face down on the floor.

Baird *rises slowly from his bunk while* **Hardie** *is doing the 51st Psalm and he sits on the floor with his legs crossed, staring blankly. After several moments he rises to his feet, he is aching, moves his legs and arms accordingly: he rubs at his eyes then covers his face and makes a yawning noise that becomes a groan: and he speaks – quietly at first but it soon becomes imbued with that breathless urgency of the opening address of Scene One, and he paces slowly . . .*

Baird I canni take this. I'm no gonni. I'm no gonni, ken cause I canni, I canni. Christ Jesus (*His head goes back and he looks upwards, sighs loudly, regaining his composure. He closes his eyes.*) Oh God, our father, please forgive me, I'm a miserable sinner, I'm without any hope; I've no to see the hills again and walk doon the field ower the back on a Sunday morning, I've no tae . . . I've no . . . Please forgive me. Oh God.

(*He clasps his hands up near his mouth, eyes closed. And then he returns to sit down on the floor in the former cross-legged posture but his legs become cramped almost immediately and he stretches his legs out, his head hangs, his upper trunk lolling forwards.*)

(*He shifts position. He starts his breathless whistling of 'Kempy's Hat'. But he stops it a moment later and hunches over again.*)

Lights out.

Scene Nine

Lights on as they were in Scene Eight.

Baird *sits in same posture.* **Hardie** *is now asleep on his bunk beneath the blanket.*

Tam *enters eventually, returning* **Baird**'s *slops pail and collecting food bowl. He peers in the keekhole, unlocks the door and enters the cell.*

He stares at **Baird**. *He sees the half eaten food in the bowl, steps closer to him.*

Tam Johnnie!

When **Baird** *still does not respond* **Tam** *grasps him by the shoulder.* **Baird** *now glances sharply at him and he jerks back.* **Tam** *is clearly relieved*:

Tam Christ man what ye doing!

Baird *does not reply but turns away from him.*

Tam Christ sake!

Baird (*slight irritation*) What is it?

Tam I thought there was something up wi ye!

Baird Something up wi me . . .

Tam Sitting there like . . . I dont know what. Whh, ye shouldni go about pitting the fear o death into folk like that – I thought something had happened.

Baird (*veiled sarcasm*) Did ye.

Tam *catches the tone and after a moment* **Baird** *shuts his eyes, then he opens them and continues*:

Baird And the military opening up wi the muskets doon at Greenock in retaliation . . . There's another ane up for Sidmouth and Castlereagh, nine folk killed – murdered. Naebody tell me that ken how come naebody tell me that! (*And he glances at* **Tam**.)

Tam I dont get to hear everything. (*Pause.*) I dont . . .

Baird Och, fuck. (*Shakes head slowly.*) Nine deid Tam; ken ordinary working folk, just ordinary working folk. It's nae good . . . it's just nae good . . .

Tam They were attacking the military!

Baird Och.

Tam They were.

Baird *frowns at him.*

Tam I'm telling ye. Truly. (*Pause.*) The soldiers were trying to escort their prisoners and then bam! a mob bloody appears from naewherr and starts attacking them. The soldiers were trying to protect no just thirsels cause a lot of the stanes were hitting inti the prisoners as well. The mob wurni even caring, they were out for blood, it was a rabble, a riot, they were rioting, right out of control, the military had nae choice.

Baird (*interrupting angrily*) I dont want to hear ye. I dont want to hear ye, your lies, aw they lies, I'm sick of aw they lies – go away, just go away, ken, back to your maisters; go away back to your maisters. Lies, just lies.

Tam (*taken aback*) It's no lies Johnnie it's what I heard, I'm telling ye true.

Baird You're telling me true! You're no telling me true. Ken you're no telling me nothing that's true! Nothing! You're just nothing! (*A tired contempt.*) You're no a man.

Tam You've got nae right to say that to me.

Baird (*pauses, then turns to him*) Aye I have, I've got the right. (*He stares at* **Tam** *for a moment or two.*) I have got the right. So's Andy, and the big smiddy; aye and Billy Clackson, Tommy Pike, auld Sandy Hart and the wee lad ken aw of us, the hale fucking twenty two – even the ither anes, the anes that ran away – we've all got the right, that's the ane thing we have got wi the fucking likes of you. (*He gazes at* **Tam**.) The likes of you Tam, aw standing back and watching ken it gies me a pain in the belly.

Tam *just staring at him; and* **Baird** *angrily slaps himself on the chest.*

Baird I'm a soldier. Dont you talk to me about opening fire on a crowd of unarmed folk with nothing bar a pile of fucking stanes, dont you fucking talk to me like that; you dont know, you dont know, I fought the fucking French, real fighting men – fucking Napoleon's men! I'm a real soldier! (*Pauses.*) Away ye go; noo; away ye go.

Tam *still just stares at him.*

Baird Go Tam, away ye go. I dont want tae talk to ye. Nane of yez, I dont want to talk to nane of yez. Never again, yir fucking lies. (*He turns away.*)

Tam *continues to stare at him, before making his exit from the cell, with the plate and the half-eaten food.*

Baird (*once the cell door is locked his head droops; his shoulders hunch and he stares at the floor. He should retain this position for full several seconds. Then he starts to remember something: he begins chuckling – in spite of himself – and he soon stops it. But he begins it again: he shakes his head. Then he grins*) My God . . . ! (*Shakes head and laughs quietly.*) I didni even see it either! I didni! I didni even see it! (*Shaking his head and chuckling.*) Ken I didni even fucking notice! (*Laughing at himself quietly.*)

Lights fade.

Scene Ten

Lights dim.

Baird *is standing by his cell door, leaning against it as if he is sleeping standing up.* **Hardie** *is lying on the floor in the foetal position. His slops pail is out by the cell door.*

Sound of rats scuffling. Then at some point a man will scream, but very distant and neither **Hardie** *nor* **Baird** *responds.*

Lights out after several moments.

Scene Eleven

Lights.

Baird *is sitting cross-legged on the floor.*

Hardie (*is reading his Bible. He pauses and gazes at the ceiling, rubs at his jaw, then speaks slowly [NB Exodus 39, verse 2]*) 'And he made the e'-phod of gold, blue, and purple, and scarlet, and fine twisted linen. And they did beat the gold into thin plates, and *cut it* into wire, to work it in the blue, and in the purple, and in the scarlet, and in the fine linen, with cunning work.' (*Frowns and continues.*) 'And the curious girdle of his e'-phod, that was upon it, was of the same, according to the work thereof . . .' (*Frowns. Chews at his thumbnail.*)

Baird *his head droops, his eyes close.*

Hardie (*again reads, enunciating every syllable*) 'And they wrought onyx stones inclosed in ouches of gold, graven, as signets are graven, with the names of the children of Israel . . .' (*And pronounces the penultimate vowel to rhyme with 'eye', then puzzled frown again and he gets to his feet and leaves the Bible on the bunk, walks downstage. Then a sudden noise from outside and he is startled, almost guilty:*

Tam *is unlocking the door.* **Granny Duncan** *is with him, the tray with two bowls of porridge.)*

Tam Morning Andy.

Granny Duncan *(handing the bowl to him)* Eat it while it's hot noo lad.

Hardie *(looks curiously at her)* Missis Duncan . . . *(He takes the bowl by mistake, then realises it.)* Eh I'm no eating this morning – eh Tam I'm no eating this morning. *(Holding the bowl to him.)*

Granny Duncan Aye well ye'd better cause there might be nane the morra!

Tam She's back making the porridge hersel now Andy.

Granny Duncan So ye'd better eat it. And while it's hot tae, nothing like a good bowl of hot porridge to fill a man. Come on now eat it up! Never know what's in store for us.

Hardie *(looks at her)* I dae but Missis Duncan.

Granny Duncan Naw ye dont son naw ye dont, ken naebody does.

Hardie *(smiles, but firmly)* I dae.

Granny Duncan *(glances at* **Tam***)* I just have to think on mysel, laid up the past few weeks and looking fit to drap aw the gether. Who'd've thought I'd ever find mysel back working again! But here I am. Here I am.

Hardie *(shakes his head at the bowl of porridge and attempts to hand it to* **Tam** *but* **Granny Duncan** *waves it away)* I'm no wanting anything the day Missis, sorry, if you've taken trouble.

Granny Duncan Naw son you've got to – ken and you've no tae bolt it, it's bad for the bowels to bolt it; you must jist take your time, take your time, and then ye'll get the benefit. *(Pause.)* And I'll jist ston here and see that ye dae.

Tam *groans.*

Granny Duncan Ah well you can jist go aboot your business Tammas Simpson, I knew your mother.

Tam So what ye knew my mother, so what!

Granny Duncan Just you go and gie that in to the other lad. And I'll see to this yin. *(Gives him a dunt in the ribs.)*

Tam *irritated movement away from her, shakes his head. But* **Granny Duncan** *gives him a fly wink, implying that she'll get* **Hardie**

to eat if left alone. He nods slightly and after a brief glance at **Hardie**
*he exits with the other bowl, locking the door behind him, and makes
his way along and into* **Baird**'s *cell.*

Baird *has still been sitting on the floor with his back to the door.
When he hears* **Tam** *he gets to his feet and walks to the end of the cell
and turns to watch the door open, and* **Tam** *enter.*

Tam Morning Johnnie.

Baird *ignores him.*

Tam It's fair bright outside this morning. (*Strolls downstage, gazes up
at the high window. He glances at* **Baird**.) Touch of damp though . . .

Baird *turns from him.*

Tam But warm mind you, still warm. (*He gazes at* **Baird**. *Eventually
he just leaves.*

When the door is shut **Baird** *walks to collect his bowl of porridge and
he begins eating quite normally.*

Meanwhile **Granny Duncan** *turns to* **Hardie** *immediately* **Tam**
leaves the cell. **Hardie** *makes to speak but* **Granny Duncan** *silences
him.*

Granny Duncan (*finger to her mouth*) Wheesht son a minute. Now
you'll no be eating your porritch the morn's morn so you'll better be
eating it this ane.

Hardie But Missis Duncan . . .

Granny Duncan (*interrupting*) Granny Duncan ye call me Granny
Duncan, that's my name, noo listen quick, you'll be writing to your
people the night cause the letters're gonni be back. He's no a bad man
Tammas Simpson though that bit ower keen tae serve them as have
the power. They tell him no tae say a word and the poor man does
jist that and if they went and telt him to cry tae the moon he'd away
and dae that tae, poor cratur that he is. Noo you sit down and write
away to your heart's content the night, eftir he's brung ye the
materials which he'll be daeing this eftirnin ken though he disni know
it yet I was telt roon the kitchen . . .
    There'll be nae need to write to please they God-fearing men that
opens your private words to your ain folk and then tears up your
private words to your ain folk if they dont meet wi what they deem
proper and fitting for ye to be saying. When you sit doon the night
tae write, you write free, ye hear? You write free. Noo yir porritch'll
come cauld and thick the morra and you dont eat it, ye jist lea it
alane, and when Tammas Simpson isni here ye turn it oot aff the

bowl and then stick your private letter in; and ance that's done ye put the cauld porritch back oan top. Noo ye understand, eh? Shh . . . (*Urgency now: the sound of* **Tam** *locking* **Baird's** *cell door.*)

Hardie Aye, but who's the letter tae go tae I mean.

Granny Duncan (*finger to her lips, interrupts him*) Wheesht noo, there's good people in Stirling . . . (*Keeps finger to lips a moment.*)

Hardie *sits quickly down, and is eating at once.*

Tam *enters. He is suspicious, but the sense that he is always suspicious of this old lady anyway. He notes that* **Hardie** *is eating.*

Granny Duncan (*winks at* **Tam**. **Tam** *nods*) I think we could just let him eat it in peace . . .

Tam Course.

Hardie *continues eating quite hungrily once they have gone from the cell.*

Granny Duncan *walks ahead of* **Tam**, *wiping her hands on her peenie.*

Baird *hears them go: he has finished eating: his bowl is on the floor. He rises, walks to the end of the cell, stretches and yawns, scratches himself, gazes upwards at the high window. He yawns again. He starts to hum a slow melody. But then he cuts it off in a bout of dry coughing.*

Lights out.

Scene Twelve

Lights.

Hardie *lies on his back. He is exercising, raising his legs alternately, then simultaneously.*

Baird (*is sitting on the floor. He is humming a tune and tracing shapes in the straw on the floor with his right forefinger. He stops and listens, then mutters*) Sounded like something, something, thought it was gonni be something, like whit, I dont know, how dae I know, I dont know – hh, I dont know . . . canni see through walls, eh how am I supposed to see through walls . . . (*He resumes tracing on the floor, and begins humming a tune again.*

(*Then he definitely hears something and gets swiftly to his feet and goes to his door and listens there*:)

The **Three Ministers** *are preceded in by* **Tam**. *They are coming to* **Baird**'*s cell.*

Hardie *also hears them and sits up. He makes certain his cell is not their destination, before lying outstretched on the floor, hands clasped behind his head. He stares at the ceiling.*

Tam (*unlocks the cell door and calls inside*) Visitors!

Baird *steps back, waiting. He folds his arms when the trio enter.* **Tam** *pulls shut the door behind them and exits.*

Dr Wright Good day tae ye Mister Baird.

Mr Heugh John. (*Said as a greeting.*)

Mr Small Good day.

Baird *unfolds his arms and turns from them, faces away.*

Dr Wright (*pause*) How are ye keeping lad?

Mr Heugh (*pause*) Are ye sleeping?

Mr Small (*pause. Murmurs*) Silence . . .

Dr Wright *nods.*

Dr Wright Are ye resting?

When **Baird** *does not acknowledge this* **Mr Small** *sighs and shakes his head impatiently.*

Mr Heugh We've put two or three books in wi the men and they'll be passed on to yoursel and Andrew in a day or so.

Mr Small (*after another silence, turns his head sharply: whispers*) This is arrogance . . . !

Mr Heugh You'll see I've marked passages I think'll be of special interest to ye.

Dr Wright (*significant look to* **Mr Heugh** *before speaking*) You're not at peace John Baird . . .

Mr Heugh Aye.

Baird *while facing away from them lowers himself down and sits on his hunkers, his knees raised, staring off from them.*

Dr Wright (*raised eyebrows to* **Mr Heugh**) Mmm . . .

Mr Small (*aside*) This is the second time now I'll remind you Mister Heugh, it's not natural behaviour.

Mr Heugh (*steps forward*) We called on Alexander Hart earlier, his head wounds have healed ye know; he sends his regards to ye. And Benny Moir is sending his to ye as well.

Baird *closes his eyes, rests his chin on the palm of his hand.*

Mr Small (*to* **Dr Wright**) He goes too far!

Mr Heugh The man's troubled.

Mr Small He's got a tongue in his heid! (*Glances at* **Dr Wright**.) He gives us no respect at all.

Dr Wright (*nods*) I'm in agreement with ye Mister Small, I must confess. (*Wags his right forefinger.*) You give us no respect John Baird, neither us nor the cloth we wear, acting as ye do. We've come out of our way to be here.

Mr Small To show you how by the grace of God you can come to terms with death.

Mr Heugh It lies in your own hands, John, the Saviour suffered death at the hands of men that our sins might be forgiven us, forgiven us by the Lord but, not by other men, by the Lord God his Father, who art in heaven.

Dr Wright The gospel has a two-fold property; it is the saviour of life unto life for those who embrace it – but of death unto death for those who reject it. If we dont abide by it for salvation, then shall it fall upon us for our everlasting destruction.

Mr Small Amen.

Baird *makes no movement. The* **Ministers** *glance at each other.*

Mr Small Your crimes Mister Baird, they're maybe preying on your mind?

Mr Heugh (*irritation*) Mister Small!

Mr Small Penitence is surely a worthy objective Mister Heugh, the man is after all under sentence of death. (*Pause.*) He has been justly convicted on two counts of High Treason.

Mr Heugh Please keep your opinions to yoursel.

Mr Small Opinions is it? Opinions – I was under the misapprehension I was stating fact. Forgive me minister, I must have been imagining things when I saw you sitting two rows in front of me at the trial. (*Turns from him to* **Baird**:) The man Wilson, James

Wilson, you must be aware he's now professing atheism; that he has actually burned a bible – burned a bible Mister Baird.

Mr Heugh (*breaking in on the last phrase*) Absolute hearsay! You go too far.

Mr Small It has been said on authority.

Mr Heugh And denied on authority. Why Dr Wright it was yourself told me Doctor Chalmers had denounced this publicly, calling it the most scandalous rumour.

Dr Wright Aye, that is what I heard.

Mr Small Doctor Chalmers's defence of the radicals is well known . . . (*To* **Mr Heugh**:) Mister Heugh, please, I too would agree that certain measures are maybe overdue but – but this past twelvemonth . . . ! The pulpit is surely the place where a minister demonstrates Christianity, not his individual political affiliations. They're after all a private affair, not something to be thrusting upon other folk!

Mr Heugh I would prefer to continue this elsewhere.

Dr Wright Aye Mister Small.

Mr Small I only point out.

Dr Wright *silences him by a swift movement of the head which also signifies they should make an exit.*

Mr Heugh (*after a pause, to* **Baird**) If you have the faith it wont be misplaced – John . . . it wont be misplaced.

Baird *does not respond.*

Mr Small (*to* **Dr Wright**) The gaoler says he doesni speak to him either.

Dr Wright (*looks at* **Baird** *and shakes his head*) You only make matters more trying for yoursel lad. But I say to ye this: dont leave it all to the last. They that forsake the Almighty shall be consumed. You must make the effort before it is too late. Have faith in him who died for us all. Through his blood salvation shall be yours. (*Signals abruptly to* **Mr Heugh** *to call on the gaoler.*)

Mr Heugh Gaoler!

Tam (*from outside*) Aye . . . (*He comes to unlock door.*)

Mr Small (*to* **Baird**) May the Lord give ye peace.

Dr Wright Amen tae that.

Mr Heugh (*to* **Baird**) There is no want of willingness in God; you must put all of your trust in Him. Nothing is beyond hope.

Baird *stares away from them.*

Exit the ministers.

Baird *glances at the door once it is being locked up by* **Tam**, *then continues just sitting where he is, gazing into space.*

Lights out.

Scene Thirteen

Sound of a clock chiming: two o'clock.

Lights.

Baird *is asleep, lying on his side upon the floor.*

Hardie (*has embarked upon the writing of 'the private letter', his account of the Battle of Bonnymuir. He reads in silence, then aloud*)
    First August, 1820. My dear friends, the following is a whole account of our proceedings to and at the Battle of Bonnymuir etcetera. I hope you will overlook any repetition of sentiment, and the manner and style in which it is written, and consider that while I was writing it I was always in fear of being discovered. I would willingly write another copy to make some improvements in the writing but I am afraid they will suspect me by getting so much paper. Let it suffice to say that it contains nothing but the truth . . .
    (*He gets to his feet holding the page and walks a few moments, then resumes aloud.*)
    On the 4th day of April we arrived at Germiston where we found a number of men in arms; and after some delay spent waiting for others to arrive from Anderston and other places, a man I did not know gave notice where we were to go and also the nature of the affair. Everything was going beyond our most sanguine hopes; he told us that England was all in arms from London downwards and that there were no soldiers to oppose our Cause betwixt there and Edinburgh. The whole country was ready to receive us!
    We were to proceed to Condorret at once and be joined there by the others. There was no one among us to take charge. The men themselves appointed me to do this and I formed them into regular order, front and rear rank, sizing them accordingly and likewise

numbering them the same as a guard. My reason for doing so: we were all strangers to one another and thus if anything were wanted might answer to our numbers. When we arrived at Condorret I found Mister Baird's house. He was expecting a party of two hundred well-armed men coming, all old soldiers, instead of which he got only us. And then we found instead of the fifty or sixty Condorret men promised we could get only five or six, though had we been more from Glasgow it would perhaps have been otherwise.

Baird *sits up.*

Hardie (*is now addressing audience directly*) Yet in consequence of this great disappointment we were not discouraged but did proceed on in most orderly manner, our first halt at Castlecarry Bridge where we got half a bottle of porter and a penny's-worth of bread each man. Our instructions were to go beyond Bonnybridge to meet with reinforcements from Stra'ven and Rutherglen and other places. We went through an aqueduct bridge about a mile onto the moor, and sat down on top of the hill, and rested about an hour, when the Cavalry made their appearance.

Baird *now gets onto his feet, casually: he strolls and halts not so far downstage as* **Hardie**, *where he will stand as relaxed as possible while* **Hardie** *continues.*)

Hardie I proposed forming a square but Mister Baird said it was better to go under cover of a dyke not far distant. We immediately ran down the hill cheering and took up position. There was a slap in the dyke there which we quickly filled up with pikemen. The Cavalry had fired a shot or two to frighten us, for they afterwards told us they did not expect us to face them. Their officer called on us to lay down what arms we had but this was not agreed to and they made an attack at the slap and got through but were kept at bay on the inside and repulsed. They then stood back, rendering our pikes unserviceable. The officer called again on us to surrender and he would do us no harm, which some of our men took for granted and they threw down their arms and ran. But those were instantly pursued and some wounded in a most shocking manner: and it was truly unbecoming the character of a British soldier to wound or try to kill any man when he had it in his power to take him prisoner, and when they had no arms to make any defence. (*He frowns, stares at the audience.* **Baird** *continues to gaze around at them also.* **Hardie** *continues, his disgust and anger quite apparent:*)

Wounded in a most shocking manner, though they had no arms to defend . . . (*Pauses, shakes his head.*)

Baird *now seems to have lost interest in the proceedings and he starts* *to whistle tunelessly, and he turns his back on the audience, goes to rest on his bunk. He lies with his hands beneath his head, staring upwards.*

Hardie After we were all brought together by the military we were taken off the moor and our wounded put into a cart – one dreadfully so – in four places I think in the head, and shot through the arm. Another old man with a frightful gash on the face – so much so that his jawbone was seen perfectly distinct. And another sabred badly on the head, and two others left for dead in the field . . .

Baird *suddenly smothers a laugh and then once more, and this time it becomes a fit of coughing, which he gets under control; and he sits now, on the edge of the bunk gazing at the audience.*

Hardie There were several others wounded but I will not say any more about them, as I suppose you have heard the particlars long before this. (*Pause.*) The Officer of the Hussars asked who our Captain was, and was his name Baird, and made it evident that some person had given them information.

We were then taken to Stirling Castle and put into one room, and being uncommonly tired it was not long before the most of us buried all our cares in a sound sleep. Mister Baird and I went to bed together but he was taken away from us shortly after and put into a dungeon, and had about four or five stones of iron put upon him. After a day or two we were all examined and on being asked why I was in arms, I told them I went out with the intention to recover my rights;

they then asked me what rights I wanted. I said annual Parliaments and Election by ballot.

Question: what reason had you to expect those? Answer: because I think Government ought to grant whatever the majority of the nation requested, and if they had paid attention to the people's lawful petitions, the nation would not be in the state it at present was – but this last part they did not think proper to put down. When I told them so they looked at one another but said nothing.

They then told me every single thing that had happened, all that had been transacted . . . (*Frowns.*) Everything. We had been deluded away. We had been deluded away. (*He lowers the paper and after a moment goes to sit, he continues writing.*)

Baird meanwhile, midway through the last paragraph, stretches out on the bunk, tugs the blanket over himself.

Sound of clock chiming.

Baird *is restless, too wide awake to sleep. He puts his hands behind his head: he begins whistling the first lines of a slow ballad but stops abruptly.*

Hardie (*begins reading the last of the letter aloud. He glances at the cell door before continuing. He speaks in a hurry to begin with, then settles into a more regular address*) As the short time allowed me is now drawing to a close I shall not give my thoughts on the Trial but shall confine myself to a few other observations. You will be curious to know what views I now entertain of those principles which induced me to take up arms.

My suffering Countrymen! As I am within view of being hurried into the presence of my Almighty Judge I remain under the firm conviction that **I die a Martyr in the Cause of Truth and Justice, and in the hope that you will soon succeed in the Cause which I took up arms to defend:**

and I protest as a dying man that although we were outwitted and betrayed it was done with all good intention, and I may safely speak for the whole of those that are here in the Castle, that they are in the same mind and all remain firm to the cause. I shall not now speak at length on the scaffold as I am a little quick in temper. Neither do I think it proper for a person so near to eternity to enter upon these matters. However, I may speak a few words. Farewell. May God send you a speedy deliverance from your oppressions is the earnest prayer of

Yours,

Andrew Hardie.

He re-reads the last section to himself and then he writes a couple of sentences on a different slip of paper [NB the same lines that are written in bold above.] And he looks around the cell before lifting his Bible from the floor by the bunk: he inserts this little slip of paper inside. He leaves the rest of the long and private letter lying where it is and he sits down on the bunk, gazing at it. He flexes his neck and shoulder muscles: he is extremely tired but at this point unable to relax his mind.

Lights dim.

Baird *rises during the last minute or so and strolls downstage looking upwards to the high window, then his gaze roams around audience.*

Hardie *now lies down, tugs the blanket over himself and tries to get to sleep. Soon he rises, and drags out the slops pail, kneels for a piss . . .*

Lights out.

Scene Fourteen

Lights.

Bella is visiting **Hardie**. **Baird** *stands leaning against the door of his cell. On top of the barrel in* **Hardie***'s cell lies the folded page of a letter he has been writing.*

Hardie (*quite excited*) See Bella she had telt me to wait till the porridge went cauld and hardened up into a lump, like a scone, so's I could just flip it oot and stick the letter in at the bottom. (*Pause. Shakes his head.*) It worked perfect. I mean it . . . (*Shakes his head.*) . . . it was just, I dont know, it was just . . . it was just so . . . (*He and* **Bella** *laugh, but not too loudly.*) And I handed the official letter tae Tam, cause I thought I'd better write ane, an ordinary ane, an extra sheet like, so's the authorities widni get the wind up – Tam himself, he woulda known, he would've got suspicious. He's no that daft.

Bella Poor Tam.

Hardie *frowns at her.*

Bella Oh I just mean he's a poor sowel.

Hardie (*rubs his forehead, chews at his thumbnail. He walks a pace, shakes his head*) It was the only wey Bella.

Bella I know that Andy.

Hardie But you're right, I didni like doing it to him. He's just a man. But they open all our letters and examine them and they dont pass them on. They've been doing it ever since we got took. And people have got to know what happened, instead of all they lies that are getting spread. It's thanks to that auld wummin the truth'll get known, that brave auld wummin . . . (*Hand to his forehead.*) Brave auld wummin . . .

Bella I hope she'll be careful though they're so awful strict.

Hardie *stares at her.*

Baird *sits slowly down onto the floor, his back to the door of his cell.*

Bella Taking chances like that, she's ower seventy ye know Andy.

Hardie (*very slowly*) Aye . . . I had to write it but . . . I had to write it . . . to get the facts out . . . so folk'll know.

Bella *nods.* **Hardie** *goes and sits on the bunk.*

Bella You're awful white looking.

Hardie (*very absently*) I'm eh . . . eh . . .

Bella Are ye no feeling well?

Hardie *gazes at her.*

Bella Andy . . . You're awful white looking. (*Pause.*) The men were asking for ye. Ye know they're awful fond of ye.

Hardie (*smiles*) The men . . . ?

Bella Aye. Uch they're in fine spirit now, since they got telt the news. Even big Jem the smiddy – you'd think he was ane of them, instead of . . . He's been put into solitary now, the same as you and Johnnie. He seems better but. It's a queer thing.

Hardie Aye.

Bella Willie Crawford says yous've no to gie up hope either, wi them being commuted there's aye got to be a chance for you, especially noo with that petition, they say everybody's pitting their names tae it – even some of the authorities. (*Her gaze drops; she is not convincing.*)

Hardie Aye. (*But also unconvincing.*) How's Johnnie Bella?

Bella Oh, quiet he's quiet . . .

Hardie *continues gazing at her and eventually she gestures at the letter on the barrel.*

Bella Did I interrupt ye writing another letter?

Hardie (*shrugs*) My relations, aye, I've got hunners of them. D'you want to read it?

Bella Och no. You're lucky having so many folk.

Hardie In some weys aye in some weys naw. (*Rises from the bunk abruptly and lifts a book from beneath it, leafs through it and finds the reference.*) About relations Bella, listen to this:

> O look not with pity's melting softness
> That alone can shake my fortitude . . .

(*Grins.*) See. Pity's melting softness, that's what shakes the fortitude. D'ye know what I mean?

   (**Bella** *is about to speak but he cuts right across her:*)
   Listen to this bit – where he's talking about being in solitary, cause that's where he was Bella, Doctor Dodds, the man that wrote it, he was in solitary the same as me and Johnnie – listen: 'Here I tower triumphant, beyond the reach of mortal hand to shake.' And this bit,

this bit was . . . (*Smiles to himself.*) . . . this bit was mysel: 'Be thy
first business here to search thy heart, and probe the deep corruption
of the mind.' Eh! Some of them dont know, the ministers, they just
dont know. (*Laughs briefly.*) Blest the dungeon which thus led to
heaven! No kidding ye Bella, blest the dungeon!

Bella Aye Andy I can see how it means what it means to ye.

Hardie (*cutting across her again*) Meditation is solitude's fair child.
(*Glances at her, shakes his head.*) Sometimes I feel as if I'm the
luckiest man in the world. None of it matters ye see, none of it. And
this is a thing only one man in a million gets to find out. And because
of that, sometimes, ye feel like you're ordained. No as if I mean like
as if you're ordained in . . . What I mean is everything happens
because it happens, because God has willed it. Evil men are as
heaven's instruments!

  Sometimes Bella I just wish I could get out of this place, to tell
folk. I feel it aw inside me ye see and sometimes I canni get to sleep
because of it, for thinking about it, and I'm wanting to jump up and
shout, jump up and shout. (*Laughs briefly and then notices that she is
looking at him and he becomes self-conscious.*)

In the other cell **Baird** *is still standing leaning against the door.*

Lights out.

Scene Fifteen

Lights: dimly in **Baird**'*s cell where* **Mr Heugh** *stands; he has been
speaking to* **Baird**. **Baird** *is sitting on the floor somewhere, turned
away from him, his knees raised and arms encircling them.*

In the other cell **Hardie** *is studying the page of a letter he is
composing. He lifts a book and leafs through it. Then he slaps himself
twice on the forehead – berating himself for something – puts down
the book. Resumes writing the letter for several moments, then studies
it and reads aloud:*

Hardie Although I am to be taken away in the bloom of life, and to
suffer an unnatural death, this gives me very little concern knowing
that he who gave me this life, can take it when it seemeth good for
him to do so; and ever blessed be his holy name, he takes but what he
gave. (*Stops and crumples the page and flings it away, smacks himself
on the head again, shuts his eyes, breathing deeply.*)

Mr Heugh (*begins to speak midway through* **Hardie**'s *last piece of letter-reading: he does so in a low voice but one that is always urgent. He is continuing a train of thought*) But if so John then you have to say it . . . God knows what's in your heart, I dont, but I feel as if I've got some understanding. True faith comes from within us, from within each and every one of us. You, with the help of the Lord, are your own agent.

(*Walks a pace and sighs.*) This world is a transient thing. There can be no faith in it, not in man, in man alone. (*Glances at* **Baird**.) Jesus says we shall be betrayed both by parents and brethren, by kinsfolk and by friends. And that some of us shall be caused to be put to death. Aye there are good men, of course there are. And you've been fortunate to know some, as I have. The men who marched with you had faith in you and it was justified by you.

Baird *shifts his position a little.*

Mr Heugh But it was. As was the faith you yourself placed in them. But faith in man John faith in man – by its very nature imperfect, coming as it does from an imperfect thing, because that's what man is, an imperfect thing. Faith in God is so totally distinct from that, because it is perfect, it comes from God, it is of God . . . And therefore must be perfect.

He stops speaking and the lights go out simultaneously. Three seconds later the lights come back on and he will continue as though no interruption had occurred.

Mr Heugh . . . you yourself placed in them. But faith in man John faith in man – by its very nature imperfect, coming as it does from an imperfect thing, because that's what man is, an imperfect thing. Faith in God is so totally distinct from that, because it is perfect, it comes from God, it is of God . . . And therefore must be perfect.

Baird *stares at him.*

Hardie *is reaching for a book, flicking over the pages.*

Lights out.

Act Two Scene One

Sound of a door thudding shut. **Baird** *is being escorted to another cell by* **2nd Gaoler** *and* **Two Soldiers** *who carry muskets and fixed bayonets, but not as if expecting trouble.*

Lights: the new double cell. **Baird***'s chains drag. He walks slowly, head bowed.* **2nd Gaoler** *unlocks the door.*

Baird *enters. He groans as the door shuts behind him and stands with his back against it. He closes his eyes.* **2nd Gaoler** *and the* **Two Soldiers** *exit to get* **Hardie***.*

Sound of a door thudding shut offstage again. Eventually **2nd Gaoler** *reappears, followed by* **Hardie** *then the* **Two Soldiers***.* **Hardie** *walks more easily than* **Baird***. His head is not bowed – but this distinction between the two should not be made too much of.*

Baird *hears the group approach. He now notices that this cell has two bunks. He stares back to the door then steps away from it when he hears the sound of* **2nd Gaoler***'s keys.*

Hardie (*steps inside*) Johnnie!

2nd Gaoler *locks the door and exits with the* **Two Soldiers** *who begin unfixing bayonets.*

Hardie (*laughs*) It is you eftir aw!

They shake hands with cheery enthusiasm. But **Baird***'s laugh becomes a coughing fit.*

Baird My throat feels like it's been scraped oot. Christ man I'm croaking! (*Lowers himself to sit on bunk.*)

Hardie (*chuckling*) What about the rest o the lads though eh! Is that no great news about them getting their sentence commuted?

Baird Aye, it is.

Hardie And big Jem as well, eftir him being telt he wisni . . . (*Walks the length of the cell and back.*) Great great news, I mean it was expected, but all the same, when it happens . . . (*Nods in emphasis.*) Eh Johnnie?

Baird Aye.

Hardie You could never've took it for granted.

Baird Not at all.

Hardie (*pacing*) The wey they went on and on aboot making examples oot o us at the trial. (*Glancing about at the new surroundings.*)

Baird (*watches him for a moment or two*) Would ye stop that marching aboot ken you're making me nervous – I've no seen such exercise for months! My ain legs man I can hardly feel them. I thought I was gonni fall doon when they were escorting me here.

Hardie Ah!

Baird Truly, it's like my whole body was numbing up.

Hardie (*nods. He puts his hands behind his head, stretches*) I've been keeping myself fit.

Baird I can see that, aye.

Hardie It's the only wey. Watch this! (*He does a fall straight down onto the floor, and immediately begins a series of press-ups.*)

Baird God! (*Laughing.*) Cut it oot cut it oot!

Hardie *continues for another two then collapses, breathing harshly, laughing at the same time.*

Baird Are ye deid?

Hardie (*getting to his feet eventually*) Doesni do to let them think they're beating us. Got to stay right. Come on! Aff your bunk and have a turn at it.

Baird No me.

Hardie Ah come on! (*Makes as if to pull him up onto the floor.*)

Baird (*hand raised to stop him*) Too tired.

Hardie Too tired, how can ye be too tired? Ye've been doing nothing for the past five month!

Baird Ken maybe later on.

Hardie Ah!

Baird I just feel like a lie doon the now . . .

Hardie *gazes at him, and nods. He sits down on his bunk.*

Baird (*glancing about*) No a bad place this eh, feels warm. Last yin I had was damp ken hell of a cauld at night sometimes, was yours?

Hardie It was a bit, aye. (*Pause.*) Ye stopped talking to folk Johnnie eh? Bella was telling me.

Baird I spoke to her.

Hardie Naebody else but?

Baird (*shrugs. He notes* **Hardie** *awaits further comment*) Uch I just couldni be bothered with it Andy. I'm . . . (*Shaking head to complete sentence.*)

Hardie What?

Baird Och . . . just . . . I'm no sure – tired . . . (*Shrugs.*)

Hardie (*after a pause*) You dont like the clergy that's come in?

Baird Ach Andy, it disni matter. (*Pause. Glancing across at him.*) No much, I suppose, naw, I canni say I dae.

Hardie (*nods*) No even Mister Heugh?

Baird sighs, *negatively.*

Hardie I thought he'd been fair, a decent kind of a man.

Baird Mm.

Hardie Ye dont think so?

Baird (*wearily*) Uch Andy I'm no too bothered talking aboot it ken if ye want to know the truth. (*Sighs. Stretches out on bunk.*)

Hardie (*looks across at him for a spell*) Ye go to church regular yourself but Johnnie – at hame I mean?

Baird (*nods*) O aye, aye, I do, aye. (*Pause.*) Ye hear what they were saying about auld Purly Wilson? Burning bibles . . .

Hardie He is a freethinker but.

Baird Aye, maybe.

Hardie Dae you think he's an atheist?

Baird I couldni tell ye, really – the ane thing I dae know though Andy I wouldni believe a word o what somebody like thon Mister Small tells me, ken?

Hardie Aye.

Baird (*yawns*) Anyhow, I thought your grandfeyther knew auld Purly?

Hardie That's a long time ago but, thirty years at least.

Baird (*settling himself out on the bunk now*) There's a boy I knew frae Stra'ven ken and he would go to auld Purly's house a lot. I went twice mysel – and I'd've went merr. They held meetings there, they had discussions.

Hardie (*frowns*) The Stra'ven men were supposed to be meeting us up by Bonnymuir.

Baird Uch aye Andy but that was what thon spy telt us! Nane of what he says can be taken like it was true.

Hardie I know that.

Baird (*coughs dryly before continuing*) I met Robert Hamilton there, at Purly's hoose . . . (*Glances at* **Hardie** *but* **Hardie** *just shrugs.*) Robert Hamilton – he was one of the provisional government committee (*pause*) like mysel.

Hardie *just gazes at him.*

Baird (*after a moment pulls the blanket up over himself*) I was telling ye about auld Purly's house ken just it was full o books and papers, periodical journals and the rest o it. They would read out bits here and there and then discuss them. Often enough the talk would go on aw night long. And then there was your fucking shift to go to in the morn!

Hardie (*relishing the idea*) Sounds fine.

Baird It was, you'd've liked it well. (*Pause.*) Ken though it's bad Andy eh what they're daeing to Purly – man o his age, he must be near sixty-five. (*Shakes head.*) Ken and then ye hear the likes o thon Small, no fit to sit at the same table wi him, but gieing out aw his lies . . . Makes ye wonder what they'll be saying aboot us, if that's what they're saying about Purly . . .

Hardie *yawns. He draws the blanket over himself.*

Baird Eh? I'm saying I wonder what sort of lies they'll be telling about us? That we're atheists maybe.

Hardie Atheists?

Baird Maybe they'll say *we're* burning bibles.

Hardie *stares across at him.*

Baird (*lying with his hands behind his head, staring at the ceiling, he smiles*) Or that we're flinging stanes at ministers! Or that we're aw taken to eating bairns for wur supper!

Hardie (*chuckles after a moment*) Their spies will be talking but. You're right. It hadni occurred to me. They'll be oot spreading their scandal. (*Almost talking to himself now.*) And folk'll be listening tae it, taking it aw in, letting themsels get tricked. Ye wonder . . .

Baird *sighs.*

Hardie Ye just wonder . . .

No response at all from **Baird** *who appears to be sleeping.*

Hardie *eventually moves onto his side. But after a time he raises himself onto one elbow and gazes across at* **Baird** *as if to ascertain whether or not he is asleep; then he takes out his Bible, opening it entirely at random. He starts to read this random verse aloud, enunciating every syllable but stops soon. He turns some more pages.*

He continues reading in silence for a few more moments then gets up from the bunk quite suddenly and slaps his brow with a frustrated groan, and he walks to the end of the cell and stands still. But he is very tense. He seems to be straining every muscle in his body, eyes shut tightly and his teeth clenched, his fingers flexing now bunching into fists.

Then he relaxes, his head hanging, his breathing comes slowly; he walks to the cell door and back again. He returns to sit down on the bunk, his hand at his forehead, covering his eyes.

Baird *gazes at him.*

Hardie (*notices after a moment*) Ye been sleeping?

Baird A wee bit.

Hardie (*sudden animation*) Heh Johnnie d'ye know Luke? That great bit in Chapter 15 where the boy goes away and lives a bad life?

Baird The prodigal son?

Hardie Aye. That's right. (*Almost as if the connection had not registered with him beforehand.*) Aye.
    It's a great bit innit! Ye see I aye found it hard. I mean I've been hearing it for years, but without truly understanding it. I used to aye feel sorry for the big brother, him that steys at hame and does his duty, then aw he gets is a row!

Baird *laughs.*

Hardie Naw but so he does. The young brother goes off to sow his wild oats and the auld yin steys at hame to do his duty by the faimly, and then what happens but the boy comes back and his feyther puts out the fatted calf.

Baird *chuckling.*

Hardie And the big brother's upset, he's upset, he's into a huff . . .

Baird Aye, I mind, he'll no go to the feast.

Hardie That's right.

Baird It's a moral.

Hardie Aye I know but as well as that, again, you've got just the idea of this one sinner getting returned to the fold, coming back to his feyther eftir being away frae him so long, in the wey that sinners return to God, even at the eleventh hour – eh Johnnie can I read it!

Baird (*pause*) Aye, course.

Hardie (*quickly turns to the page, and he walks a pace or two, speaking while he does so*) His father spies him in the distance and rushes out and kisses him and . . . (*Now reads*:) 'And the son said unto him, Father, I have sinned against heaven, and in thy sight, and am no more worthy to be called thy son. But the father said to his servants, Bring forth the best robe, and put it on him; and put a ring on *his* hand, and shoes on *his* feet: And bring hither the fatted calf, and kill it; and let us eat, and be merry: For this my son was dead, and is alive again; he was lost, and is found.'

Baird (*softly*) Aye.

Hardie (*smiles*) And then further on where he tells the big brother . . . (*And reads*:) 'Son, thou art *ever* with me.' *Ever*! (*Grins.*) Ever and always. He's never got any reason to worry at all, he should just be glad of somebody else getting led back into the fold.

And that's it because God takes greater pleasure in one sinner being redeemed than aw the rest of the righteous arriving up in heaven – and how no! because they're aye with him anywey, they're never away – it's nothing against them, it's just that he *knows* they're coming! (*Closing Bible.*) I used to think it was something against them, I used to think the sinner was the best, but he isni, he's no the best at aw, he's no anything, he's just the same, except he's been lost, who art now found. (*Shrugs.*)

I'm the eldest in my faimly. Relations Johnnie I've got hunners of them, wee brothers and sisters and cousins, nieces and nephews. What about yoursel?

Baird I've got three sisters, two brothers – you met ane of them, Rab, at Condorret, mind? him that telt us aw tae stoap hame and forget about marching tae Carron! (*Chuckles.*) He aye had a good head on his shoodirs the same man. A good brother tae. With me and him the roles are a bit the opposite frae the prodigal ken it was aye me that went a-roving wi him the wee brother steying at hame.

Hardie (*chuckles*) Ye call being in the army seven year 'a-roving'! (*Returning to sit on the bunk.*)

Baird (*laughs*) Aye, well said!

Hardie The 95th you were in?

Baird The Rifle Brigade, aye.

Hardie Did ye like it?

Baird Eh, I'm no that certain that I didni, in some weys, I suppose – what about yoursel?

Hardie A wee bit. (*Frowns.*) No being under fire.

Baird Aye ken being a soldier'd be great if it wisni for the fucking fighting!

Hardie (*chuckles; now lies on bunk, resting on his elbows. A pause before he speaks*) Were ye never merrit Johnnie?

Baird Nah no me.

Hardie No me either. I have a lassie but. Her name's Margaret, Margaret McKeigh – Maggie. (*Glances across.*) She's fine, fine. We hadni says about getting merrit but . . . but we baith knew, we knew.

    Black hair she's got, she wears it done up the back, in a kind of bow. (*Chuckles.*) It looks good so it does. Her neck, it shows her neck off, she's got a really fine looking neck. That sounds daft, does it?

Baird Naw.

Hardie (*smiling*) I dont know what it is; it's maybe it's like a bird, ye know the neck o a bird? the wey it slopes . . . ? (*Does the hand movements in illustration.*)

Baird (*smiling*) Aye.

Hardie I met her brother afore I met her. (*Pause.*) I wisni her first, her first boy. He died. He had a bad chist. Just young tae it was a shame. The two of them . . .

    It disni bother me . . . (*Glances across.*) Maggie having a lad afore me, it disni bother me.

Baird Uch naw for God sake.

Hardie Naw but I think it would some people, I think they would think maybe it means ye wurni her true love. I dont see it that wey but. The boy that died, I see him just as a . . . just as a boy that's deid.

Baird (*pause*) Is she aulder than ye?

Hardie Naw, younger.

Baird (*nods, continues after a moment or two*) Cause there was a wummin I went wi . . . back in the army days. I met her doon on the coast – I mean right doon ken in England, not far frae Plymouth. She was aulder than me a fair bit. She had two bairns, a wee boy and a wee lassie. I was supposed to go back ance the war finished . . .

Hardie (*waiting for him to continue, sees he is not going to*) Tell us.

Baird (*shrugs*) Uch naw.

Hardie Come on.

Baird (*shrugs*) Just – I aye wondered if I was a feyther by her Andy see I used to stey wi her quite reglar. Ken they didni mind much at the camp. She worked on a fairm and I skipped oot tae her eftir hours. I used to meet her outside the barn – aw the women workers were kept in a barn the gether. They kept their bairns there wi them as well . . .

Middle of summer it was, hot nights; sticky, you aye felt like going for a swim, even eftir midnight. We did tae, quite a few times. It was something special, ken? Truly. Something special . . .

(*A few moments pause.*) Nah, I wouldni be speaking right if I says I had a hatred o my time in the army.

And eftir it was aw over and done wi, when we aw came hame: nae work, nae hoose, nae food, nae nothing – I would like to've gone fucking back ken straight back in.

As well as that, my feet'd got the itch. I hated being hame, stuck there at that bloody web! Whh! Tell ye something man it used to get me so's I thought o doing something unlawful and getting took for it, just to get transported, to get sent overseas – right away aw the gether! Van Diemen's Island. Van Diemen's Island. Even the name, I'd go there for the name alone!

Mind you if I *had've* got took – wi my luck – they'd've fucking hanged me! (*Chuckles. Then suddenly serious.*) God's truth Andy see if they were to commute my sentence I'd really thank them. I'd . . . What! I must be getting saft in the heid – thank them! Dear God I'd get right down on my bended knees, my bended knees, I'd get right down on my bended knees!

Hardie *makes no response at all to this. Both men now continue resting on the bunks, staring into space.*

Baird (*covers his face with his hands, but only for a moment. He glances across*) The British soldier Andy, for the past twenty year we've been destroying liberty wherever we find it, right across Europe – Italy, France, Germany, Spain – sticking tyrants into power. Ye wouldni credit it, wherever we find freedom we fucking destroy it. Just fucking goats so we ur, a herd o fucking goats!

Like this time as well, getting taken in by a handful o judases . . .

(*Covers his face for a moment, then angry frustration and smashes his right fist twice on the palm of his left hand.*) I should've fucking known but I should've. I should've fucking known. And when yous turned up – twenty handit! Twenty! Man we were expecting two hunner! Two hunner: aw ex-soldiers! What a fucking laugh thon turned oot to be!

Hardie (*clears his throat*) It disni matter.

Baird I dont mean the lads were bad either cause they wurni. They just – they wurni soldiers, ken? You served Andy, you know what I'm talking about.

Hardie (*shakes head*) It disni matter; none of it.

Baird (*sarcastic*) Six thousand men landing frae Paris, Kinloch of Kinloch and the French. And Marshall MacDonald. Ye hear about him? How he was supposed to be coming tae! Marshall MacDonald! I shoulda known, he must be near ages wi Granny Duncan. (*Shakes head.*) My brother Rab tae he was suspicious frae the start. Even before yous turned up, it was that yin King, the spy, mind him? There was something just no right aboot him, he was maybe too nervous . . .

Hardie None of it matters.

Baird He couldni sit at peace ken he kept jumping about and going to the door . . . couldni look ye in the eye.

Hardie (*pause. Ironic chuckle. Pause*) My grandfeyther says I shouldni have went either. But ye know how? The rain. He says it was an omen, the worst rain he'd seen for forty year.

Baird The rain!

Hardie Naw but from that Sunday we first saw the Proclamation tacked up doon by the Cross it never stopped, a downpour, merr or less right through till eftir we'd got to Bonnymuir – five days solid, sheets of rain, just sheets of rain. (*Lapsing into silence.*)

Baird (*sighs after a while, puts hand over his face, and groans*) Aw Rab Rab . . . Aye been the same, back since we were bairns the gether.

Hardie (*gazing upwards*) Never seen anything like it! Five days, solid . . . just sheets o it.

Baird Hoping something would come along . . . But what was there could come along, nothing, there was nothing, I should've known that ken I should've known . . . What in God's name did I hang aboot for, aw this while, there was nothing tae haud me back, I shoulda packed the bags and went . . . (*Slowly shaking head: a glance across now to* **Hardie** *who listens to him*:) Christ man if I could get back oot o here I'd never go hame. Condorret! Naw, no me, never, never again. (*Shuts eyes, teeth clenched.*)

Hardie (*smiles briefly*) Liberty isni worth having if it's no worth dying for . . . (*Pause.*) We swear to return home in triumph, or not return home at all . . .

Baird *Eyes still shut.*

Hardie (*seriously, quite loudly*) Equality exists in the Bible and must exist in the state.

Baird (*chuckles and clenches right fist*) Scotland free or a desert.

Hardie (*loudly*) Whenever an aristocracy exists so too does oppression and misery.

Baird (*shouts*) Freedom or slavery.

Hardie (*shouts*) Privilege of birth overrides justice and truth. The right of the people to resist oppression must always exist.

Baird (*now laughing*) You know aw the best anes.

Hardie (*also laughing*) A man's a man for aw that.

Baird For aw that an aw that.

Hardie Wee sleekit coorin timorous beastie!

Lights out.

Their laughter continues for a few moments: fade on it.

Scene Two

Lights dim.

Hardie *sleeps on his bunk, turned to the side away from* **Baird** *who is sitting on the floor, drawing shapes in the straw, humming an unintelligible tune.*

Two Authorities *enter and approach the door of the cell, and they stare in through the keekhole.* **Baird** *stops what he is doing and stares at the keekhole.* **Two Authorities** *soon exit.*

Baird (*eventually tilts sideways and allows himself to fall onto the* *floor, and he lies like this, wide awake, still humming the unintelligible tune. Then he stops it and comes in on the following verse before the chorus of 'Rising of the Moon'. He sings quietly and slowly*:)

> for the pikes must be together
> at the rising of the moon.
> At the rising of the moon
> At the rising of the moon
> For the pikes must be together
> at the rising of the moon.

(*He breaks off, still lying sideways on the floor, eyes open and wide awake.*)

Sound of a clock chiming the hour five.

Baird (*speaks when the echo has died*) Cinque.

Lights out.

Scene Three

Lights dim.

Hardie *is seated on the floor, downstage, his Bible lies close to him; he is listening to* **Baird** *who is standing with his back to the cell door.*

Baird (*in the midst of narration*) My maw's cousin that was. Her man and his neighbour had a boat ken quite a big yin I seem to mind though I'm no sure the actual size o it. Used to catch wur supper out the water. Big cod and a wad of mackerel mainly it was: the mackerel we hud fur breakfast but for during the day it was the cod we ate.

Me and my brothers used to go oot with them at the crack of dawn. My uncle – that's whit we cawed him – him and his neighbour took us hail, rain or shine.

Silence everywhere, that's what I mind, the sound of the water lapping against the side of the boat. We let the lines dangle over the edge.

They aye took us tae the same spot. Ken tae start wi. It was right across near to Bute. That's on the nor-western side but the wey it is sometimes when you're fishing, ye look up and find you've been drifting . . .

(*Chuckles.*) Then back to the house and we'd fill wur bellies, then away trekking round the shore, playing for miles along the coast, swimming tae – I mind this great big palace of a place, I dont know whose it would've been; auld Argyll himsel I dare say, it was built like a castle and on three sides surrounded by a right fucking thick forest, the other side facing doon ower big bushes and rhododendrons, doon to the water's edge; us hiding frae the keepers – they'd've fucking shot us ken bairns or no – if they coulda catched us! Ah they'd never've catched us though, no ance we hit the shore man we could sprint ower the tap of the rocks and the stanes like we wur a perra wild beasts, wi never a foot wrang . . . (*Laughs.*)

Pause.

Hardie*'s head and shoulders droop: difficult to tell whether he has dozed off.*

Baird (*after several moments reverie*) Aye, I suppose, I suppose she was a noisy wummin . . . (*Grins.*) But I aye liked that. Ken and I liked her singing tae. I learned her some o oor songs. She had this English voice, a right English voice, ye know the wey some of them ur Andy – oi oi oi, oi oi oi – that was the wey it was, her voice. But I liked it, I liked hearing her. Cause I'm a dour kind of filla in a way I suppose I have to admit, so huvvin a cheery wummin like Annie, my God though it was fine. She'll be thirty-seven or merr noo. And the bairn, ten year auld near enough. Ten. (*Frowns.*)

Hardie *is still in former position.*

Baird (*eventually, continuing from another reverie*) And he took his belt tae us. Tae me I should say – I was aye unlucky that wey, he never seemed to catch anybody else – I was nae good at dodging ye see. (*Chuckles.*)

Then that first time I came hame and he saw me for a soldier – ho! he looks me up and doon. Aye, he says, you're a bit big for the belt noo. Aye feyther, I says.

I could still pit ye on your back but.

I believe ye could feyther, I says. (*Shakes head, smiles.*) Wi maw deid though it didni maitter anymerr. That was the thing ye see, eftir she passed on the fire went oot him, it just went oot him. And that was a funny thing for me tae see cause I wouldni've thought it possible. See him noo, sits on his cherr by the grate aw day, sterring at nothing. Eighty year auld . . . (*Stares at the floor.*) Ach the faimly'll take care of him, they'll see him fine.

Hardie *now looks up at* **Baird**, *waiting for him to continue, but instead of doing so* **Baird** *turns and frowns at his bunk then lies down.* **Hardie** *returns his attention to the floor and he draws shapes there with his finger. Then he reaches for his Bible and begins to read.*

Baird *draws the blanket up to his chin, he lies staring at the ceiling, wide awake.*

Lights fade out.

Scene Four

Sound of **2nd Gaoler**'s *key in the lock simultaneous to lights on fully.*

Hardie *stands downstage while* **Baird** *sits on his bunk, knees drawn up, resting his elbows on them. Both awaiting the visitors: the* **Three Ministers.**

During the scene each of the trio, and also **Hardie,** *will occasionally glance at* **Baird** *as though to include him in the conversation. Except where otherwise directed* **Baird** *ignores them and gazes at his feet.*

Mr Small Good evening to ye.

Dr Wright Good evening. (*He seems quite tired.*)

Mr Heugh Good evening Andy, John.

Hardie Good evening.

Mr Heugh How are ye?

Hardie Alright.

Mr Heugh The company, for ye both, it must make a difference?

Hardie It does, aye. (*To* **Dr Wright,** *indicating the bunk.*) Would ye rest yoursel **Doctor Wright**?

Dr Wright Eh I'll no lad, no the night, thanks aw the same.

Mr Small Your friend here Mister Hardie, we were given to understand he'd regained the use of his tongue.

Hardie *frowns at him.*

Mr Small We were advised he had found his voice. (*Shakes his head, glances at* **Dr Wright** *and they both look to* **Baird.**)

Mr Heugh (*to* **Hardie**) And are yous managing to rest at all?

Hardie (*pause*) I thank God for the relief he affords us.

Mr Small And continue to do so. True rest canni be found outwith the arms of the Lord.

Dr Wright Mr Small speaks truly lad. (*Addresses them both*:) Yous must pray and pray and pray again. And when yous're aching, when your limbs are greeting out at ye for rest, ye just get down on your knees and ye start praying again. Yous must give thanks to God for sending his only begotten Son down to us, through whom alone we can be saved, by the shedding of his own pure blood. Yous must pray. And yous must repent.

Mr Small And dont think ye can leave it to the last. Ye must fight to reconcile yoursels wi God now, now!

Mr Heugh God himsel will grant ye strength for the battle though. He will. Have faith in him, for he wont let ye down. (*Glances at* Baird.) He wont let ye down.

Dr Wright John Baird, God will grant ye baith the strength if ye but open yirsel to him. But ye must allow him to succeed, ye must allow him to strengthen your purpose.

Mr Heugh Have faith in him John, as Andy here has. If in nothing else you must have faith in him. Even at this late hour.

Mr Small Repent. Both of ye. Ye must repent.

Hardie *stands with head and shoulders bowed.* **Baird** *is staring at his feet again, knees drawn up and his elbows resting on them.*

Mr Small (*brief shake of the head while looking at* **Baird**) *Ex uno disce omnes!*

Mr Heugh Mister Small . . . (*Glances from* **Dr Wright** *and back.*) Please keep your remarks to yourself, the man is . . .

Mr Small *In limine mortis* Mister Heugh, aye, well then, let him be ever mindful of it – let them both be ever mindful of it.

Baird *looks at* **Mr Small** *for a moment, then back to his feet again.*

Dr Wright Ye baith have less than one week in which to make your peace with God. (*Glances at* **Mr Heugh**.) This canni be gainsaid, it has got to be impressed upon them, the enormity of their predicament.

Mr Small (*to* **Dr Wright**) At times they seem as if they're no even aware of it!

Dr Wright (*does not respond to* **Mr Small** *though he has heard his comment. He addresses the* **Prisoners**) Dont hide the truth frae yoursels, yous've got to face up to it, for only then will ye find comfort. Ye must seek your peace in God through the blood of his only begotten son.

Mr Small There's less than one week! Less than one week! Think on it, think on what it means.

Dr Wright Not till man submits to Christ, not till he puts away all confidence in himself but in him, can he hope to serve the Lord God.

Mr Small He whose affections are set upon the world is living in the delusion of idolatry.

Mr Heugh Where do we get our faith but by the hearing of the word?

Hardie Aye but surely men come to God in different ways?

Dr Wright That's as maybe but in the end there is only the one way, the one true way.

Mr Heugh (*nods*) The routes are many and diverse through which we discover faith, routes we might well seek to regard as our own invention but what remains unalterable is the fact of that faith. It is one thing, it comes through God and Christ Jesus. True faith is one thing and one thing only, it is perfect.

Mr Small (*wagging his finger at* **Baird**) There's no hiding from him. He knows all within us. If we pretend to faith God knows and rightly chastiseth. We can justify oursels to oursels and to others; but God alone knoweth our hearts. That which is highly esteemed among men is abomination in the sight of God. Whosoever exalteth himself shall be abused . . .

Pause. Then lights out.

Three second pause and lights on.

Mr Small (*wagging his finger at* **Baird**) There's no hiding from him. He knows all within us. If we pretend to faith God knows and rightly chastiseth. We can justify oursels to oursels and to others; but God alone knoweth our hearts. That which is highly esteemed among men is abomination in the sight of God. Whosoever exalteth himself shall be abused . . .

Baird *stares at* **Mr Small.**

Hardie (*finishing off the quotation*) . . . and he that humbleth himself shall be exalted.

Baird *glances at* **Hardie.**

Mr Small (*to* **Hardie**) Aye. And consider it well. The both o ye. He that exalteth himself, that sets himself and his kind up to subvert the constitution and Government of the country by law established.

Baird *slowly covers his eyes with one hand, in an undemonstrative* *way, but it is enough to stop* **Mr Small** *talking, then he reaches to draw out his pail, and with his back to the company and to the audience, he urinates.*

Mr Small *sighs and shakes his head.* **Hardie** *wearily puts a hand to his forehead.* **Mr Heugh** *sighs, shakes his head.* **Dr Wright** *just stares at* **Baird.**

Baird *finishes and adjusts his clothing while kneeling with his back to the others, then he replaces the pail, and he lies down on the bunk with his hands beneath his head, gazing upwards.*

Hardie *walks to the other end of cell and stares at the floor.*

Dr Wright John Baird. Ye're a sorry sight . . . (*A glance at* **Mr Small.**)

Mr Small (*goes to the cell door, thumps it once*) Gaoler!

Dr Wright (*nods. Contemptuous*) A sorry sight. (*Walks to stand by* **Mr Small** *by the cell door, then it opens and they exit.*)

Mr Heugh (*urgently*) It does ye no good John, no good whatsoever, ye canni drive everything out, ye canni suffocate your own mind. I'm disappointed in ye, ye just allow them . . . by your actions . . . ye just allow them . . . (*The* **Gaoler** *awaits him and he breaks off, he exits at once, and the cell door thuds shut.*)

Baird (*closes his eyes and begins chuckling quietly. But he soon stops it and remains silent. Then he raises himself to call to* **Hardie**) Never seen such a quick leave-taking in aw my born days – eh! See the faces! (*Brief laugh. But* **Hardie** *is not responding.*)
Ach. I had nae choice! What was I supposed to do? Eh? What's up wi ye? Something wrang? Eh?
They've got nothing to dae wi me! Nothing. Ye hear me! State-paid clergy, they've never had nothing to dae wi us, wi liberty, nothing! Aye the very opposite. So dont look tae me!
What right have they got to tell us to repent? I've nothing to repent for ken nothing. I've done nothing I'm ashamed of. On the one hand you say everything we done was for justice, freedom and truth – for aw that we believe in and haud sacred – the next thing ye turn roon and start to repent. Repent! For what? These . . . people – coming in here! Coming in here . . . (*Becoming incoherent.*)

Hardie *is silent.*

Baird Hear me, they sent James Lapsie into auld Purly's prison cell.

Hardie I know that.

Baird (*contemptuous*) The Reverend James Lapsie from Campsie –

him that spied against Thomas Muir back in the auld days ken that's
your clergy for ye, trotting along to do their maisters' bidding ken
berating Purly to repent, repent! But what is it they've been truly
seeking? – a confession! a fucking confession, that's what Lapsie's
been sent in eftir, a confession, on behalf of his lords and maisters,
Sidmouth and Castlereagh, the whole damn shebang o them! Cause
how? Cause they're wanting rid o Habeas Corpus ken that's how,
they're wanting rid o it, they're wanting to be able to suppress us
wioot the fucking inconvenience o it being borne witness tae in
public.

   (*Both he and* **Hardie** *stand gazing at each other for a few moments,*
then he continues.)
   Are ye ashamed of how we're here? Eh? Is that how you're
wanting tae repent your crimes? Repent your crimes. Aye Andy,
that's the thing, that's what they're looking for: and a fine piece it'll
make for Colonel Hunter and his *Glasgow Herald.* (*His contempt*
palpable) Radicals repent of their wicked ways. Radicals confess of
their crimes. O, whit crimes? Oh! The anes that they *undoubtedly*
intended tae commit!
   (*Wearily.*) Ah the cant Andy, aw the cant, and the lies, aw the lies;
lies, lies, lies and merr lies – frae the judases.

Hardie (*a pause before he speaks*) Nobody forces them to come.
They huvni been sent in in the wey you mean. I dont believe it. I
know what you're saying. And I know as well about what they're
doing to auld Purly in Glasgow. (*Turns abruptly.*) But that doesni
make aw clergymen the same. You've never heard the likes o Doctor
Chalmers Johnnie he's stood up there on the pulpit and he's spoke
about reform – he's defended the radicals, he's spoke out in our
favour. Manys the time. And I've heard him. I've been there myself
and heard him wi my ain ears.

Baird *wipes his brow, agitatedly.*

Hardie He has, truly.

Baird *nods.*

Hardie They come a great wey here. I'm no gonni say anything
aboot Mister Small. I'm no gonni. But . . . Mister Heugh's helped me;
it's him put us in books and gave us talk these past long weeks and
months; if it wisni for that . . . Being able to read, just being able to
read . . . I dont know what'd've happened wioot it, what I would've
done I think I'd've went daft – daft, I think I'd've went daft, wioot
seeing the Word, if I hudni been able to see the Word.
   I'm no repenting for marching. I'm no ashamed of nothing we
done. It's just that we're aw sinners. All of us. We're sinners. And I

canni get away frae that, it's no a thing I'm able to deny, that I'm a sinner. Cause that's the wey we are, aw of us, we're aw sinners.

Baird *nods.*

Hardie We are. The ministers as well, they're nothing special. Everybody's a sinner. Everybody. We're born into it. And Jesus saves us. It's only through his grace that we even get the chance o repentance. Without him there'd be nothing at all. He took our sins on his own head. Through his blood the whole sinful world is saved.

Baird (*quietly*) I know that.

Hardie It's only through him we see it isni all a waste of time. All this world Johnnie it's nothing, just a cheat; born out of sin and in sin till it comes to God. Ye can see it, ye look aboot and ye can see it. Transient. It's a cheat, it's just a cheat. One minute you're free and you're alive you're free and you're alive, you think you're free and alive. And then you're deid. You're deid.

   I canni . . . get away frae that. (*Gazing at* **Baird.**) I'm no repenting for marching. I was wanting to fight for what's right. I'd aye dae it. I've aye done it . . .

Baird I know that.

Hardie *stands with one hand to his brow.*

Lights out on the two men staring at each other.

Scene Five

Lights.

Hardie (*closes the Bible and takes a letter he has been writing from the floor beneath his bunk. He returns to sit on a different part of the floor. He stops writing and reads in silence for several moments, then he rises and walks a pace. He reads aloud, in a quite subdued fashion*) My dear and loving Margaret, Before this arrives at your hand I will be made immortal and will be, I trust, singing praises to God and the Lamb, amongst the spirits of just men made perfect, through the atoning blood of our Lord and Saviour, Jesus Christ, whose all-sufficient merits are infinitely unbounded.

Baird *at this point opens his eyes but lies as still as he can, as though taking care not to reveal he is now awake and hearing the letter read.*

Hardie I hope you will not take it as a dishonour that your unfortunate lover died for his suffering and insulted country. I know you are possessed of nobler ideas than that. I took up arms not to rob or plunder, but for the restoration of these rights for which our forefathers bled and which we have allowed shamefully to be wrested from us and I trust the innocent blood that is soon to be shed will awaken my countrymen from that lethargy which has so overcrowded them.

But this is not a very pleasing subject to you, so I will leave it, and direct your attention to matters of more importance. We are, one and all of us, lost and miserable sinners and have to stand before a great and just God who is infinite and pure, and who cannot look upon sin but with the utmost abhorrence; it is only through the blood of a crucified Saviour that we can expect mercy at this awful tribunal.

I will be under the necessity of laying down my pen now, as this must very soon go out. You will give my dying love to your father and mother, James and Agnes, Mrs Connell and Jean Buchanan. I hope you will call frequently on my distressed and afflicted mother. Farewell my dear Margaret, may God attend you still, and all your soul with consolation fill, is the sincere wish of your most affectionate and constant lover while on earth. Andrew Hardie.

(*He scans the pages a bit uncertainly then he relaxes, takes the letter and lays it on the bed. He returns to sit down on the floor with his Bible, opens it and begins reading at random. Then he shuts it and lays it on the floor. He closes his eyes and clasps his hands as though in prayer. Then he relaxes the posture and sits with his head and shoulders drooping, as though exhausted.*)

Baird (*eventually raises himself up onto his elbows. He speaks softly*) Ye dont get hardly any sounds here Andy, have ye noticed that, it's so awful quiet. That last cell I was ye used to hear aw kinds of noise, rats scrabbling roonaboot, and through the night ken you'd aye hear screaming.

Hardie *covers his face with both hands; he could well be crying but he makes no sound other than that his breathing is a bit louder than usual.*

Baird Did auld Granny Duncan tell ye that story about the lions? (*No response from* **Hardie**, *and he continues:*) It's no anything really, just some auld King of Scotland that steyed in the castle used to keep lions down here, it was kept as a place for beasts o the jungle – ken I think ye can smell it a wee bit dae you? (*No response.*)

Hardie (*takes his hands from face*) How are they no gieing us visitors, they should be gieing us visitors. There's folk coming to see us and they're no letting them in. My grandfeyther coming aw that wey and maybe other folk tae.

Baird Aye.

Hardie They should be gieing us visitors, how're they no gieing us visitors. (*Pause.*) Eh? Ye think even Bella I mean how come she's no even getting to come? Ye think she'd be here. (*Pause.*) Eh?

Baird *still not responding.*

Hardie (*sitting round to face him*) Eh? Eh Johnnie? (*Pause, gets up from the floor.*)

Baird (*clears his throat*) Sometimes you're better aff wioot visitors Andy. Ye dont ayewis want to be seeing folk . . .

Hardie (*absently*) I'll have to write to them aw, tae everybody. (*Frowning.*) It's a duty, it's incumbent upon me.

Baird Ye dont have to write to everybody, no if ye dont want tae.

Hardie Aye but I've got to tell them (*pacing*) they've got tae know how I am, the wey I am, the wey things are – I dont want them putting theirsel to concern about me.

And nae merr petitions or that, it's pointless, better look to God and no waste their time. And they've to stop hoping the sentence'll get commuted, there's nae time for it.

(*Stops pacing.*) It disni matter anywey, none of it, none of it at aw. It's through him they'll get their peace. They've no to worry aboot me – aboot us – we'll be wi him. It doesni matter that they mangle wur body cause they canni mangle wur soul. He gave us our being; we are subject unto him; and he can call us to his glorious presence whenever he sees it meet. The ministers are right in that wey. However painful our trials and afflictions may be we are assured he worketh to reconcile these whom he loveth to himsel.

Baird Aye.

Hardie And we dae come to him in our own wey. They're wrang therr. They've maybe no worked it out.

Baird They've no had tae.

Hardie We are at all times under sentence of death. (*Pacing again.*) Even when we're in the midst of life, when we think we're free to dae whatever we like, we're no, for God takes when he thinks fit, just like he gives. He gives and he takes whenever he thinks fit, and who are we to question. We accept and we understand. It's just like aw the wee weans that get cut down before they've had the chance o living properly. Take my ain faimly, my maw, her six wee yins that died, just fell sick and died, afore even they'd really a chance of life. That's how me! (*Surprised smile: stops pacing.*) Blest the dungeon which thus led to heaven. (*Sudden frown.*) I mean being able to make my peace through the Saviour . . . There's no many granted the privilege. Eh Johnnie, the baith o us, eh, there's no many granted the privilege, truly, when ye think aboot it.

Baird Aye.

Hardie How vain are all the hopes of man. He cometh forth like a flower and is cut down.

Baird *is gazing at the ceiling.*

Hardie Dust we are and unto dust we must return. (*He returns to sit on the bed, stares at the floor.*)

Baird (*eventually calls to him*) You were saying about the stars earlier on Andy . . . (*Pause.*) Eh Andy . . . (*Pause.*) Getting oot among the hills, ken away frae Glasgow.

Hardie Aye . . . (*Glances at* **Baird**.)

Baird (*pause*) Naw, jist . . . ye want a bit o life now and again, the peace and quiet's aw very well, but ye need a bit o life. Condorret was aye deid ye see, unless somebody was maybe getting merrit or something. Naw, I think Glasgow mighta suited me better. Or Paisley, I aye had a wee fancy for trying Paisley. Some good folk there, plenty o talk.

Hardie I thought ye were fed up wi talk, I thought ye were wanting away aw the gether. Van Diemen's Island, what aboot Van Diemen's Island?

Baird Aw tae hell wi Van Diemen's Island.

Hardie (*smiling*) That was whit ye telt me . . .

Baird Did I? Aye, suppose I did – but ye shouldni believe what I tell ye Andy. I'm notorious. Ye should talk to Rab aboot that. Ye never know what I'm doing – neither do I myself ken I dont even know myself, what I'm doing. That's aye been my problem. Rab's different. So are you, you're different.

Hardie Naw I'm no.

Baird But ye are, ken, ye are, ye're better than me.

Hardie (*irritated*) Ach Johnnie that's daft talk, come on.

Baird (*shakes head*) I knew it back when yous came that night. One of the chief reasons how I went I think, I didni want to let ye doon . . . (*Frowns.*)

Hardie *sighs. He does not like hearing this.*

Baird When I saw yous standing oot in yon downpour, drenched tae the fucking skin – Christ yiz looked in a bad wey! (*Chuckles briefly, then serious.*) But then you sized them into rank. Ye did! And then marched them – ye *marched* them! (*Chuckles.*)
    That was how I knew ye had done your time in the airmy. And eftir listening tae Rab aw night it was a sight for sore eyes, ken it wis, truly. I really felt, ach, proud, proud!

Hardie I was the only soldier apart frae a couple of the auld yins right enough, that was how they had wantit me to take command. I was glad to haun it ower tae you but. Ah Johnnie they were good though, the lads. Eh!

Baird Aye they were good. Mind the Lieutenant at the Trial? Says he wouldni've known we wurni a regiment. A regiment by God! (*Chuckles.*) Aye – the only honest man in the court so he was. And tae think I nearly fucking killed him! Did I tell ye that?

Hardie Naw.

Baird Ken when he rode oot yon time and asked us tae surrender. Mind? Wee Benny telt him tae fuck off! (*Brief laugh.*) When he was riding back though, that was when I aimed at him; I had him deid tae, in my sights. It was the correct course to take. But I couldni pull the trigger. I couldni. (*Glances over at* **Hardie** *who is non-committal.*) I couldni. (*Shakes his head.*) Soldiers! They dont even know what they're fighting for.

Hardie Ye canni blame them.

Baird Aye ye can. There's too much been happening. They're killing their ain people, and well they know it.

Hardie Och aye but Johnnie it's no like that at the time, no when you're there and it's happening roonaboot ye.

Pause.

Baird Ye canni make sense o it.

Hardie What?

Baird. Nothing. (*Sighs.*) A few days afore we got pit in the gether I tell ye man I was away wi it, I hardly mind any o it at aw, any part o it – lying oan that bunk listening to the wattir drip doon the waws, and the rats scuffling away in the coarnir, that poor cratur screaming aw the time, it wis horrible; I was in a state; I dont know – ken? It wisni even like a nightmare it was as if I was away somewhere else in my fucking heid, away at some place inside it and I was just looking oot, the outside bits of my heid were shielding me from what was going oan, like it was a cave and therr wis me trapped inside – naw! no trapped, it wisni like that, I was just fucking inside, out of it aw, from what was going on roonaboot ken if maybe Tam or the auld wummin was in gieing me a bit of food man I've no had yon feeling afore, that I can mind, no even frae being a bairn

and I've often thought nothing happens to ye but that it happened tae ye when ye were wee, in some wey or another. But no like this, that being alone by yirsel man I've never had any feeling like it, ken I dont think anybody'd understand less they'd fucking had it thirsel, eh? (*Glances across for a response.*)

Hardie *nods.*

Baird Did you feel that Andy?

Hardie (*pause*) A bit.

Baird I asked Bella about the screaming, if she knew who it was, cause in a queer way it didni strike me that it was a person daeing it, I just thought it was like (*shrugs*) just a scream, frae naewherr.

Hardie (*after a moment*) Who wis it?

Baird A bankrupt, just a fucking bankrupt. (*Chuckles.*) God's truth!

Hardie (*a deep sigh*) Aw Johnnie I'm no finding it easy when ye blaspheme, I know ye're no meaning it, but I'm no finding it easy, wi somes o the things ye say, I'm awful sorry. (*Gazes at* **Baird**.) Wi respect tae ye and dont be offended.

Baird *Stunned. He lies outstretched, stares at ceiling.*

Hardie I'm awful sorry.

Baird Aw . . . (*Puts hand to his forehead.*)

Hardie Dont be offended. Eh Johnnie?

Baird (*after a moment*) Naw.

Both men lie gazing at the ceiling.

Hardie Hey Johnnie, I wrote some lines out frae Doctor Dodd, d'ye want to hear them? (*Glances across but* **Baird** *is not responding.*) Eh?

Baird (*after a moment*) Aye.

Hardie (*gets his papers from beneath the bunk and rifles through them for the page, and he walks downstage, talking as he goes*)

Be thy first business here to search thy heart
And probe the deep corruptions of the mind.

(*Brief laugh*.) I used to think o him a lot Johnnie, lying in his
dungeon doon in London. Never less alone than when alone. That
was what he says about solitary; Never less alone than when alone.
(*Smiles, and then he reads, facing back to* **Baird** *who continues to lie
gazing at the ceiling*:)

Cheerfully my friend oh! look not thus
With Pity's melting softness! That alone
Can shake my fortitude. All is not lost.
Lo! I have gain'd, on this important day,
A victory consummate over myself
And o'er this life a victory. Oh this my
Birthright to Eternity – I've gained
Dismissal from a world, where for a while,
Like you, like all, a pilgrim passing poor,
A traveller, a stranger, I have

Lights out abruptly mid-sentence.

Scene Six

Lights: dimly. Both men are in their bunks, under the blanket.

Baird (*as though in midst of conversation*) I dae like a piece of fish
but – ken?

Hardie So do I.

Baird Aye but man, I should never a telt thon wummin I liked the
herring, it was a mistake I regretit for the next six month. (*Both men
chuckle*.) See it wis the bones caused the scunner first, I just kept
seeing my haun go up to my mouth, picking them out ane by ane,
laying them oan the plate, then the knife going back up with the next
bit, then going back doon and the haun going up for the bones,
picking them oot and laying them doon, the whole thing ken
horrible, bones, fish and knife; bones, fish and knife – and then
sometimes your fingers bump into your lips, ye ever had that?

Hardie *laughs abruptly. Then* **Baird** *also laughs, but more subdued.*

Baird *gets out onto his feet and stretches. He strolls downstage, lowers* *himself to sit down on the floor and begins drawing shapes in the straw, whistling to himself. Eventually he starts to sing under his breath, (unintelligibly) still drawing the shapes in the straw. He stops after a time; he stares at the floor.*

Hardie (*opens his eyes: begins speaking, still staring upwards*) He gives it sense. I couldni imagine how it would be without him it would just be a nonsense, it would be a nonsense, wiout him, it couldni be borne, nane o it, it couldni.

Baird (*softly*) Aye.

Hardie That's how ye know it's a cheat, the injustice, the suffering, ye'd go daft if ye sat doon and just thought aboot it aw, the wey things are.

Baird (*quietly*) They've never gave us nothing wioot it being wrested from them, never. We've aye had to fight. Every bit o progress, it's had to get tore aff them, they'd have gave us nothing if we'd left it to them – nothing.

Hardie *lies staring at the ceiling.*

Baird (*after a while*) Andy . . . about Bella . . . it was me, I telt the gaoler no tae let her come. It wis nothing to dae wi the authorities. It was me. Ye see it was getting so I didni think mysel able to bear it, if she did come, I couldni have stood it at aw, I couldni've.

Hardie (*eventually murmurs*) Aye . . . (*His eyes close.*)

Baird She's that young. She shouldni be here, no in this place. What they daeing letting her here, for suchlike work, us having tae see her, in this place.

Pause.

Baird (*softly*) Hey Andy. (*Looks across to see* **Hardie**'*s eyes are shut.*) Andy, ye sleeping? (*No response.*)

Lights out.

End